Giovanni Boldini:
Masterpieces in Colour

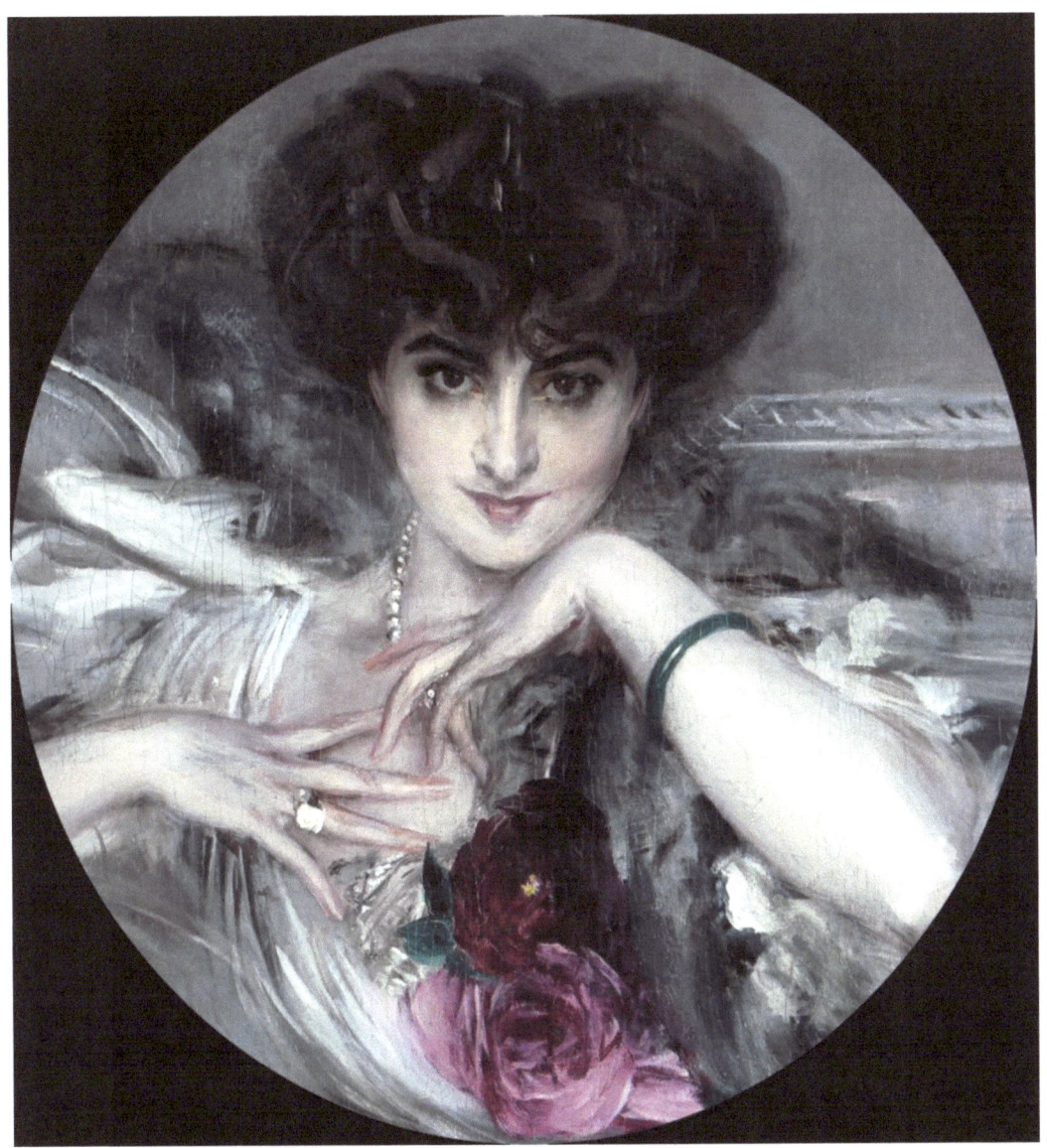

By Jessica Findley

First Edition

Foreword

Giovanni Boldini enjoyed a long and successful artistic career. According to a 1933 article in Time magazine, he was known as the "Master of Swish" because of his flowing style of painting. His paintings showed his subject in soft-focus, elongated, in movement, alive, and sophisticated. The brush work on his paintings was swift and bold. It is the masterful brushwork that gives his paintings the sense of motion. Boldini painted mostly portraits and also landscapes in the naturalistic style of his day, influenced by the Macchiaioli schooled artists he knew in Florence, and worked on engravings, with pastels, watercolors and etchings.

Boldini was born in Ferrara, the son of a painter of religious subjects, and in 1862 went to Florence for six years to study and pursue painting. He only infrequently attended classes at the Academy of Fine Arts, but in Florence, met other realist painters known as the Macchiaioli. Their influence is seen in Boldini's landscapes which show his spontaneous response to nature, although it is for his portraits that he became best known.

Moving to London, Boldini attained success as a portraitist. He completed portraits of premier members of society including Lady Holland and the Duchess of Westminster.

From 1872 he lived in Paris, where he became a friend of Edgar Degas. Boldini developed his own, distinct style, and his portraits grew in fame, helped greatly by a portrait commissioned by Giuseppe Verdi in 1886, the biggest celebrity of his day. He was nominated commissioner of the Italian section of the Paris Exposition in 1889, and received the Légion d'honneur for this appointment.

Boldini's style of painting shows some Impressionist influence but most closely resembles the work of his contemporaries John Singer Sargent and Paul Helleu. Only toward the end of his long life, did his style change, using mainly dark, rich colors.

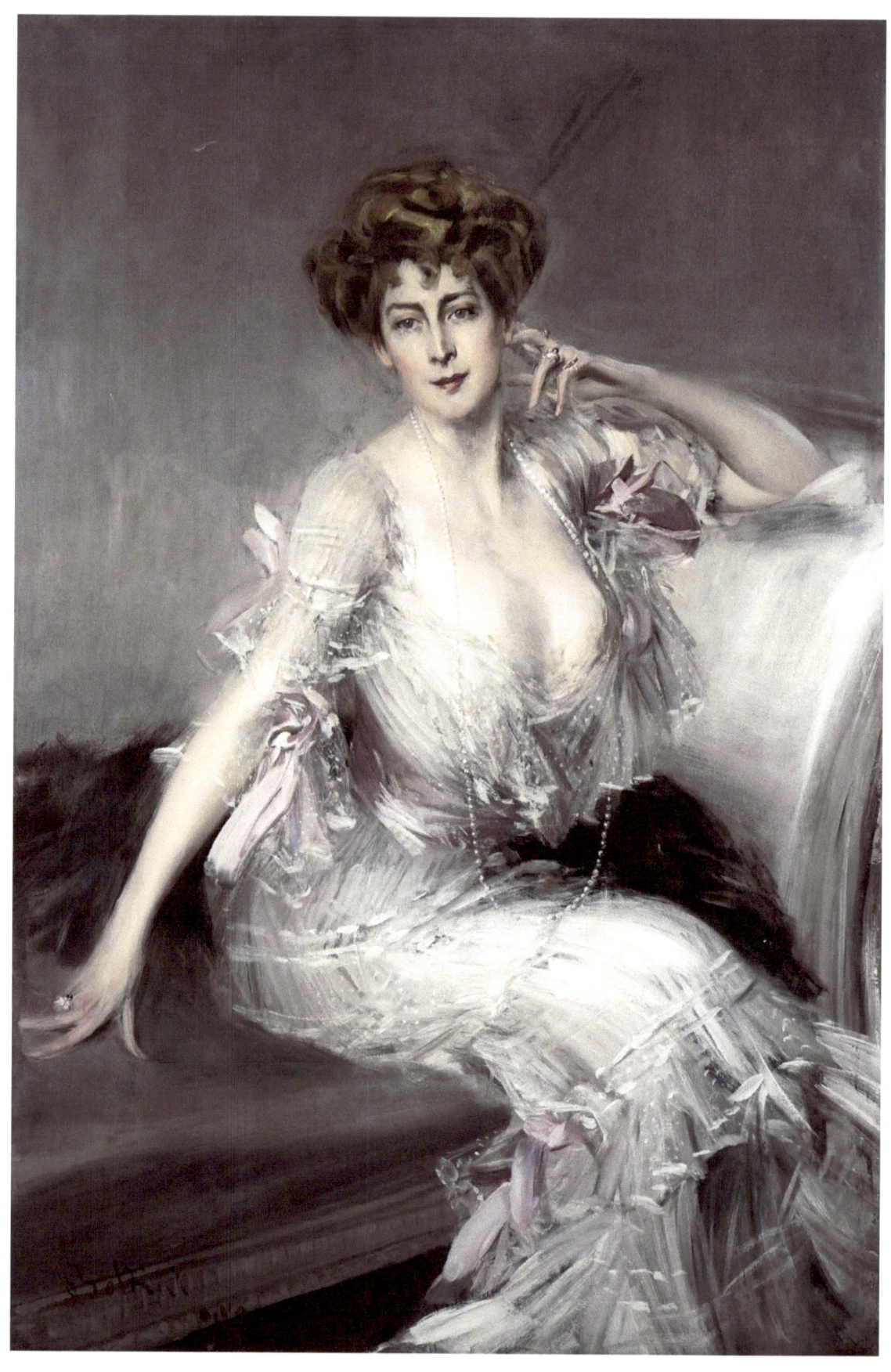

Portrait of Anna Elisabeth Hansen
Oil on canvas, 144 x 98.5 cm

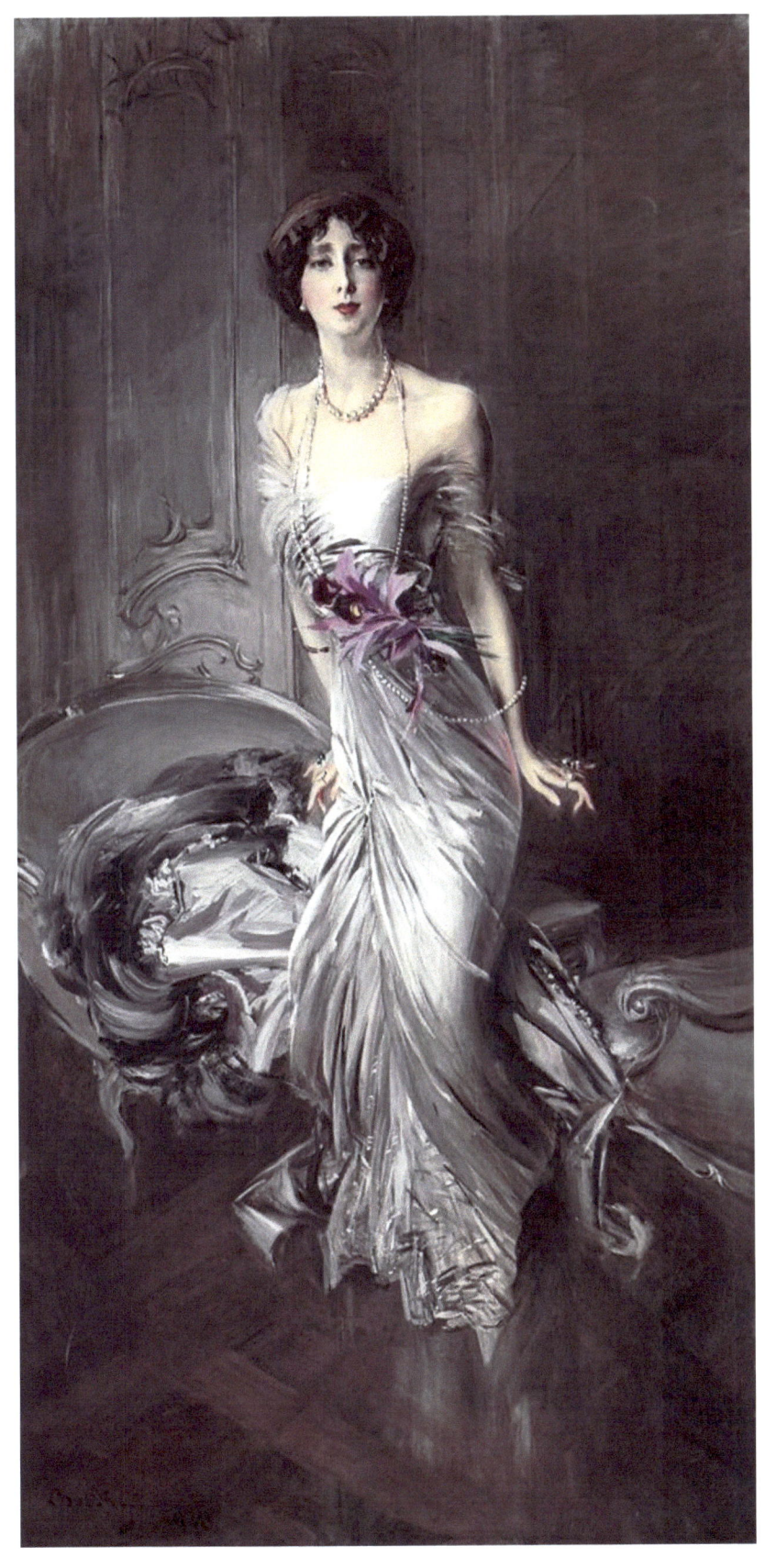

Portrait of Madame Eugène Doyen
1910, oil on canvas, 224 × 112.4 cm

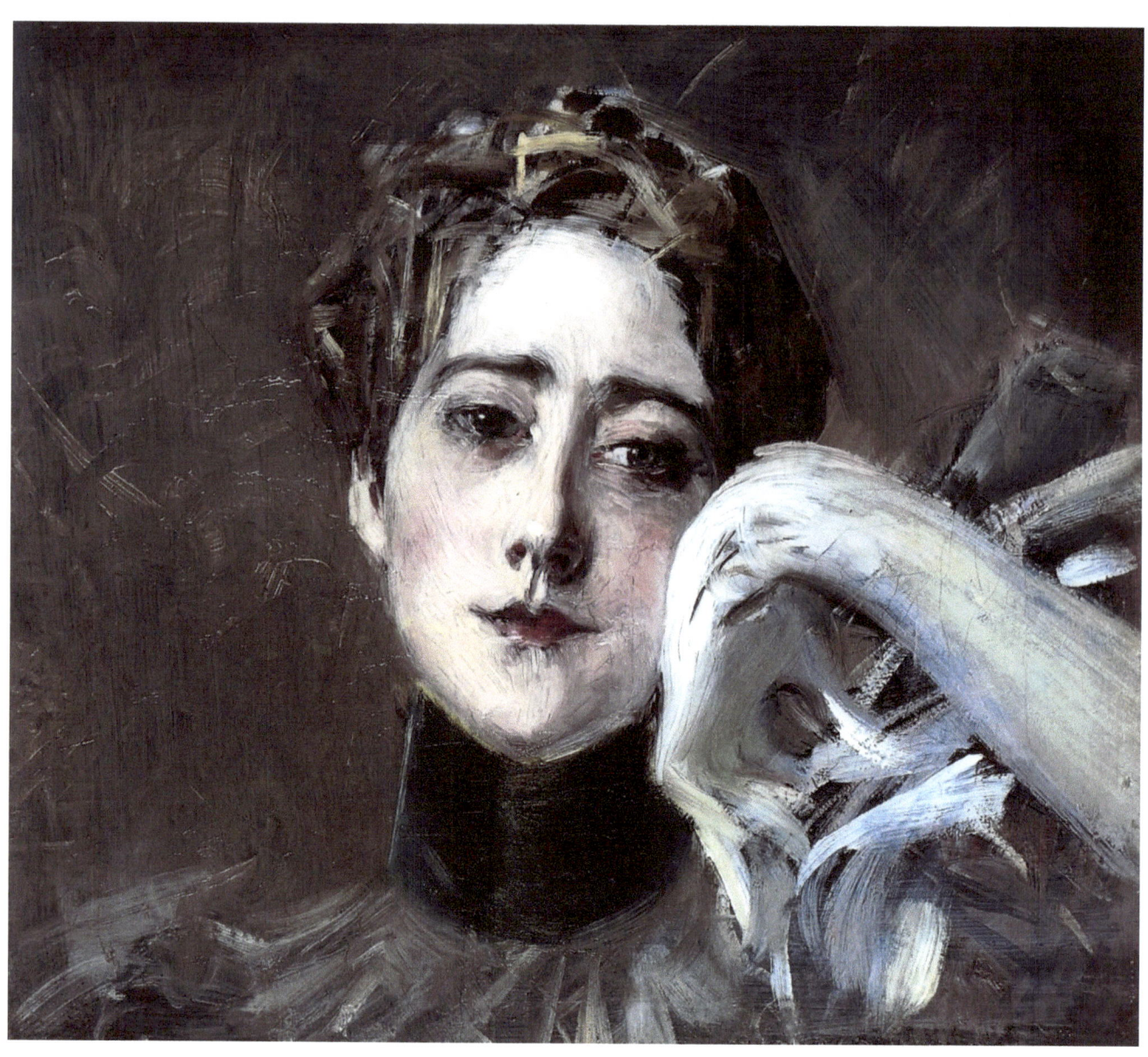

Portrait of Princess C. d'Isemburg-Birstein
1896, Oil on canvas, 37 x 41 cm, private collection

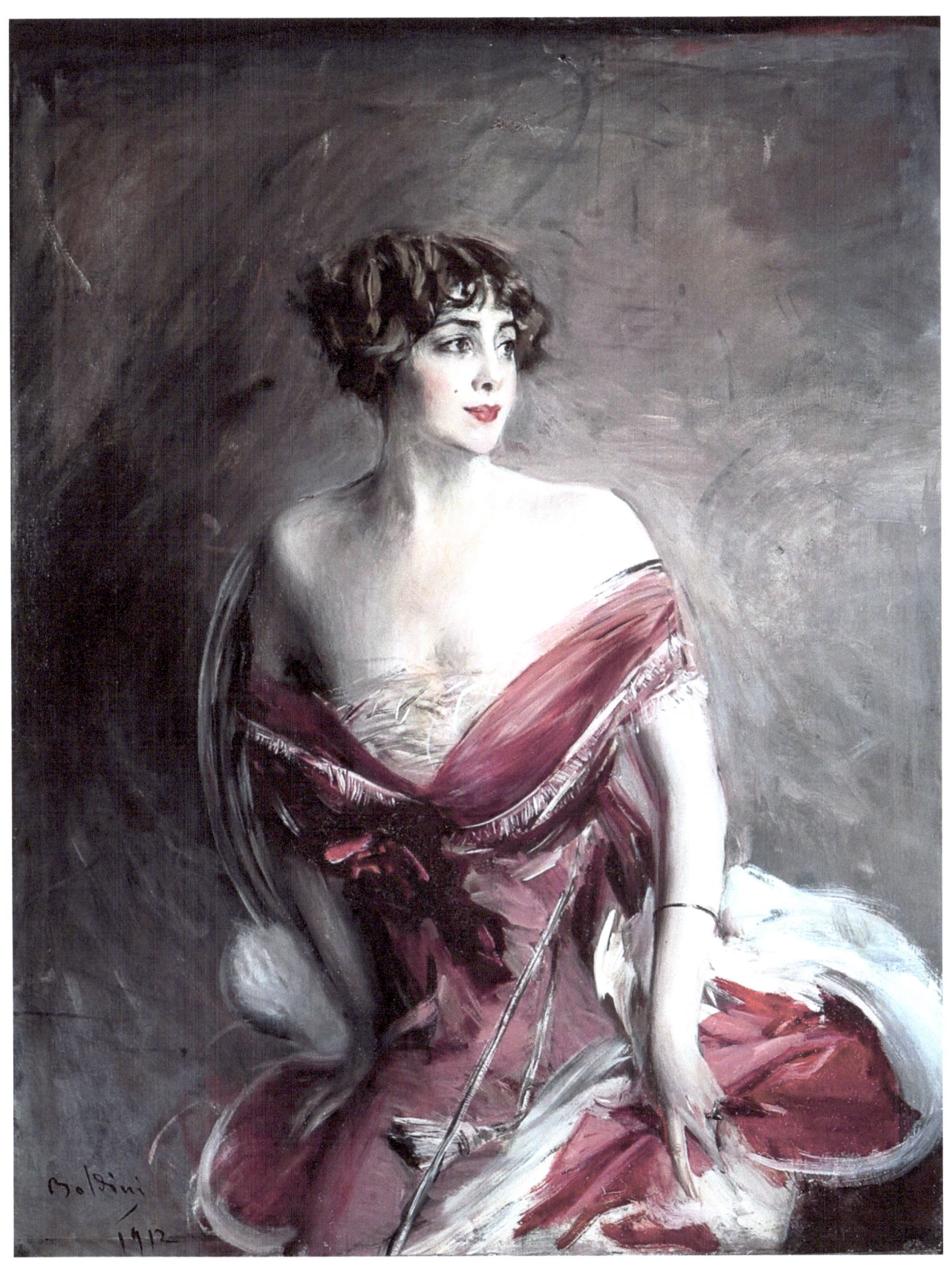

Mademoiselle De Gillespie (La dame de Biarritz)
1912, Oil on canvas, 130,2 x 97,2 cm, Private collection

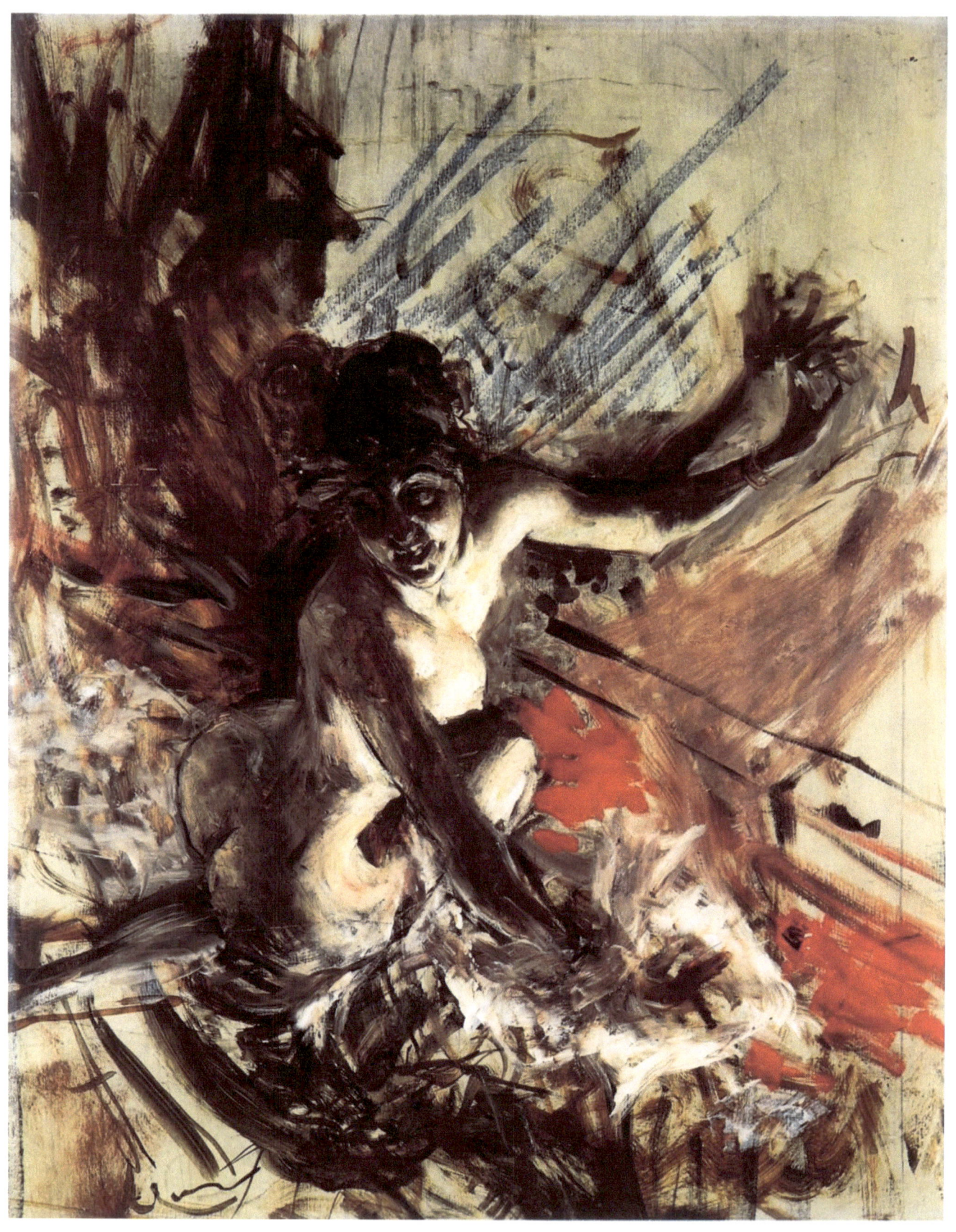

Radiant smile, Madame de Joss
1905, oil on panel, 75 x 60 cm, private collection

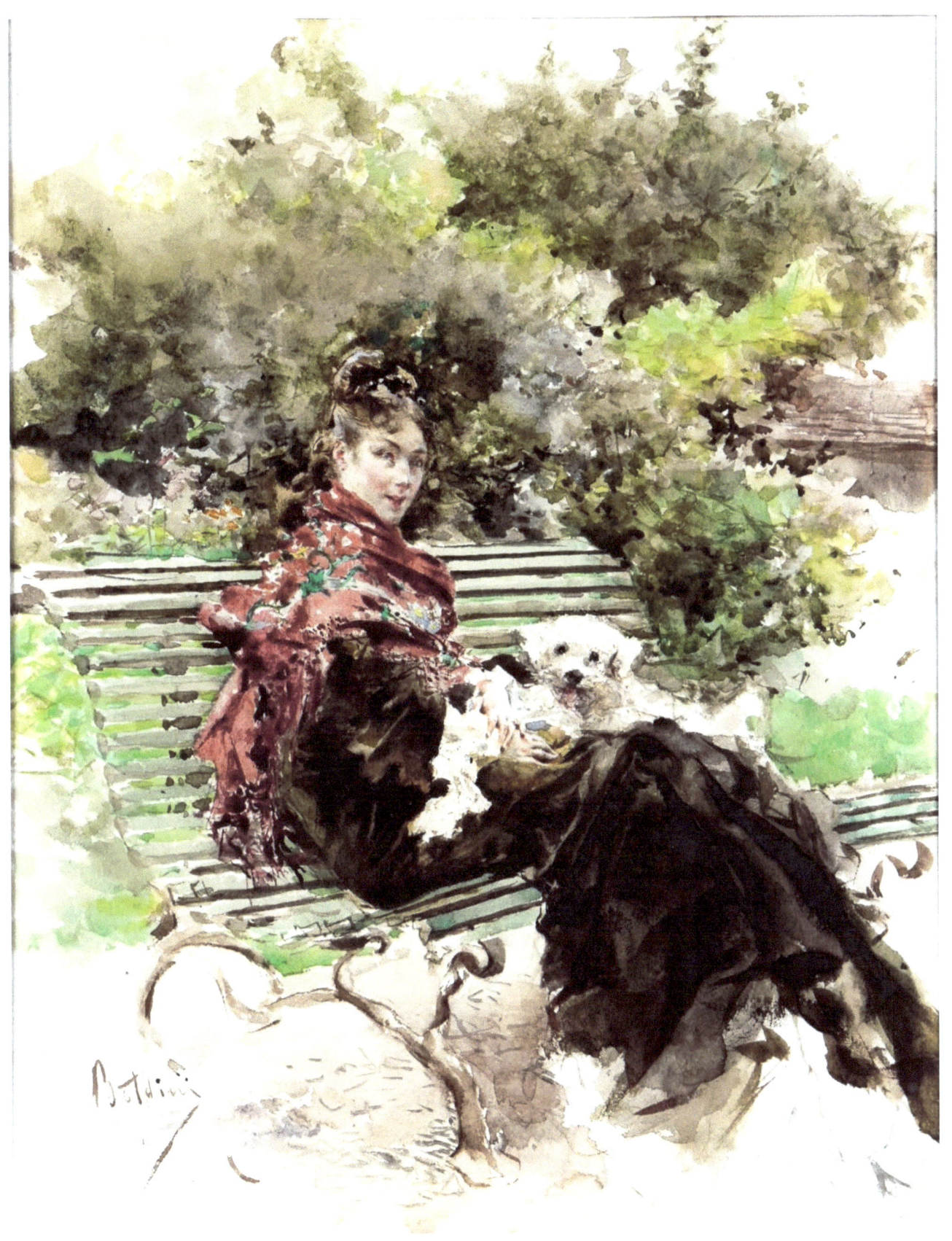

In The Park

1872, watercolor on paper, 387 x 307 mm, Private collection

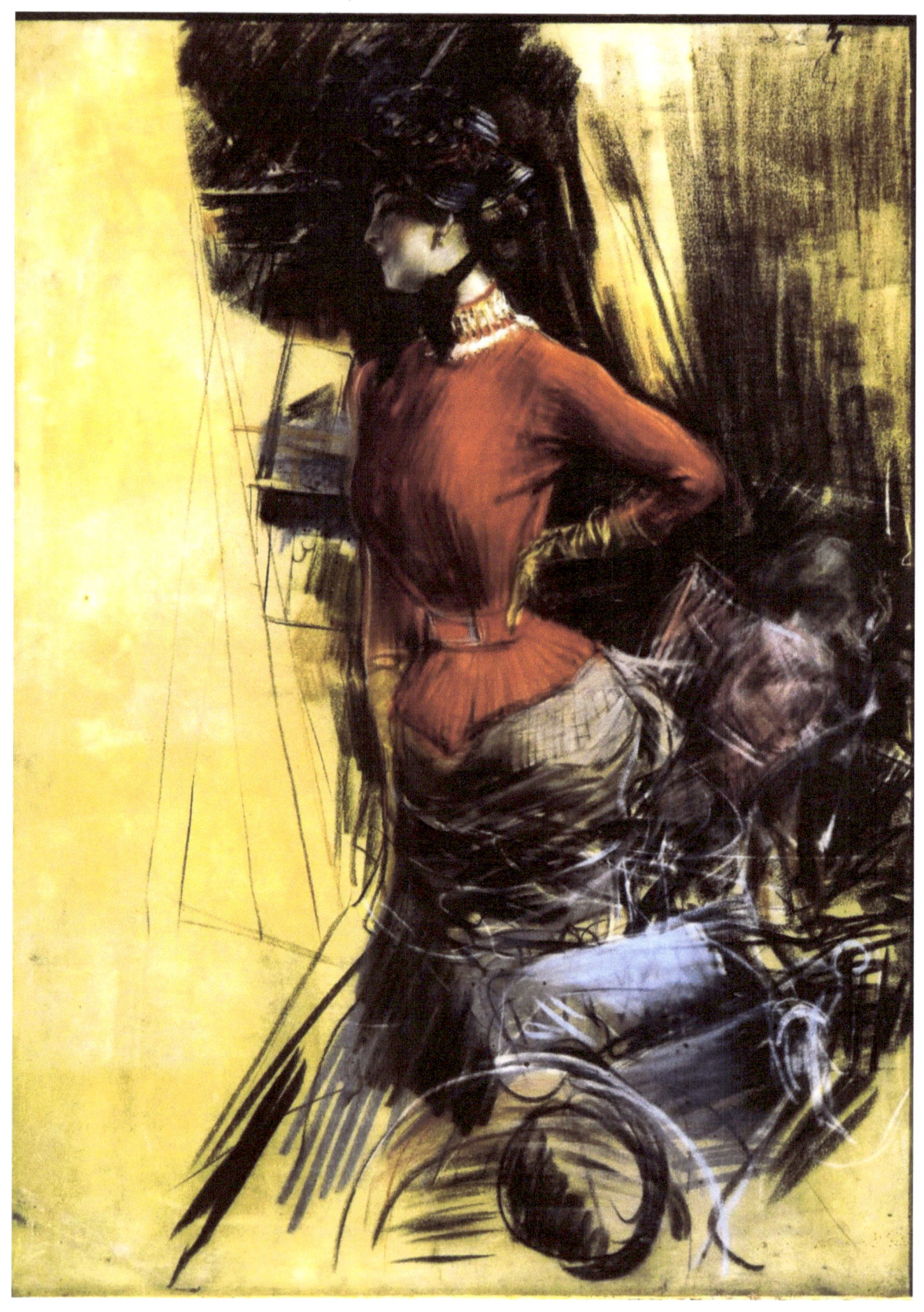

Lady in red jacket,

1878, Pastel on paper, 100 x 73 cm, private collection

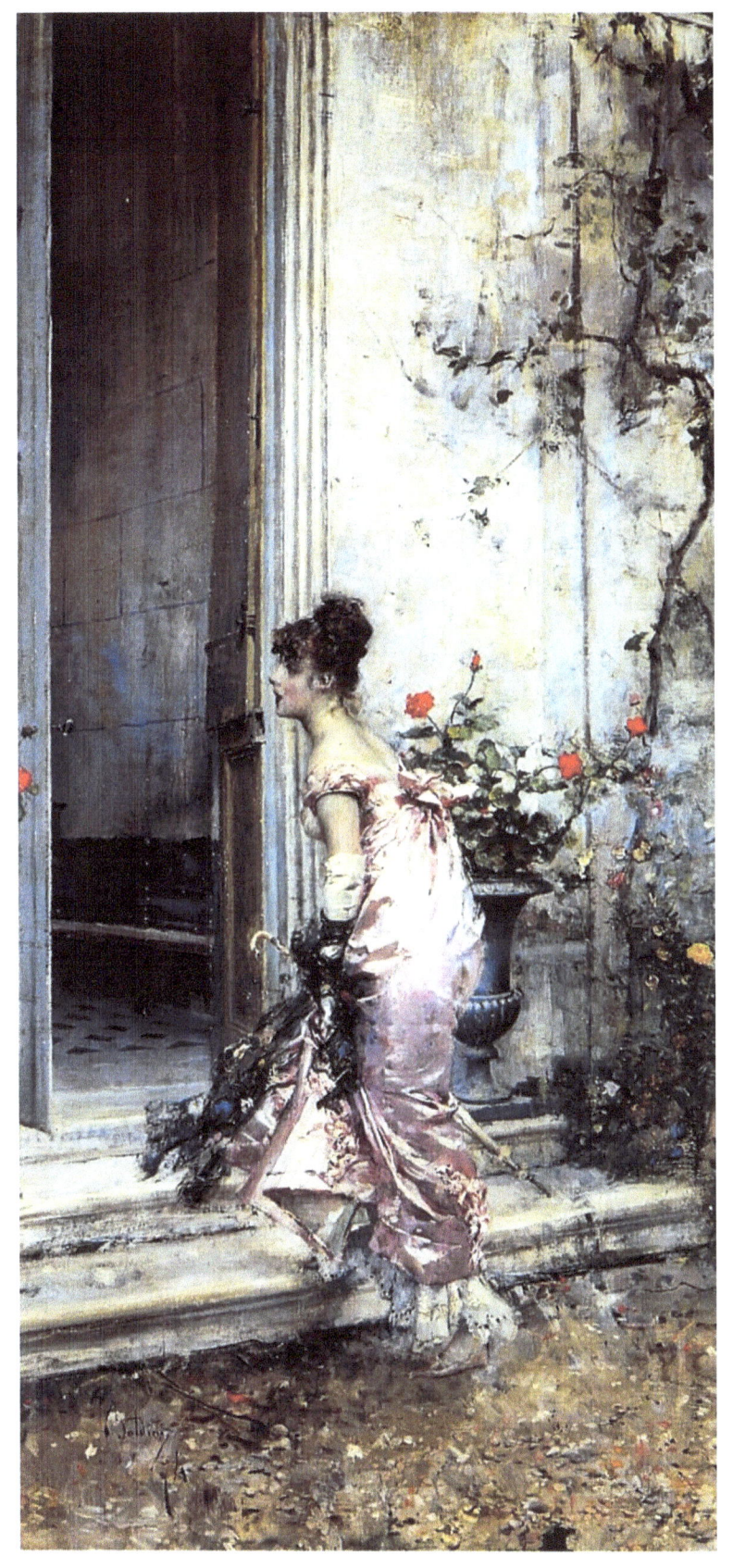

The Visit

1874, oil on panel, 79 x 38 cm, private collection

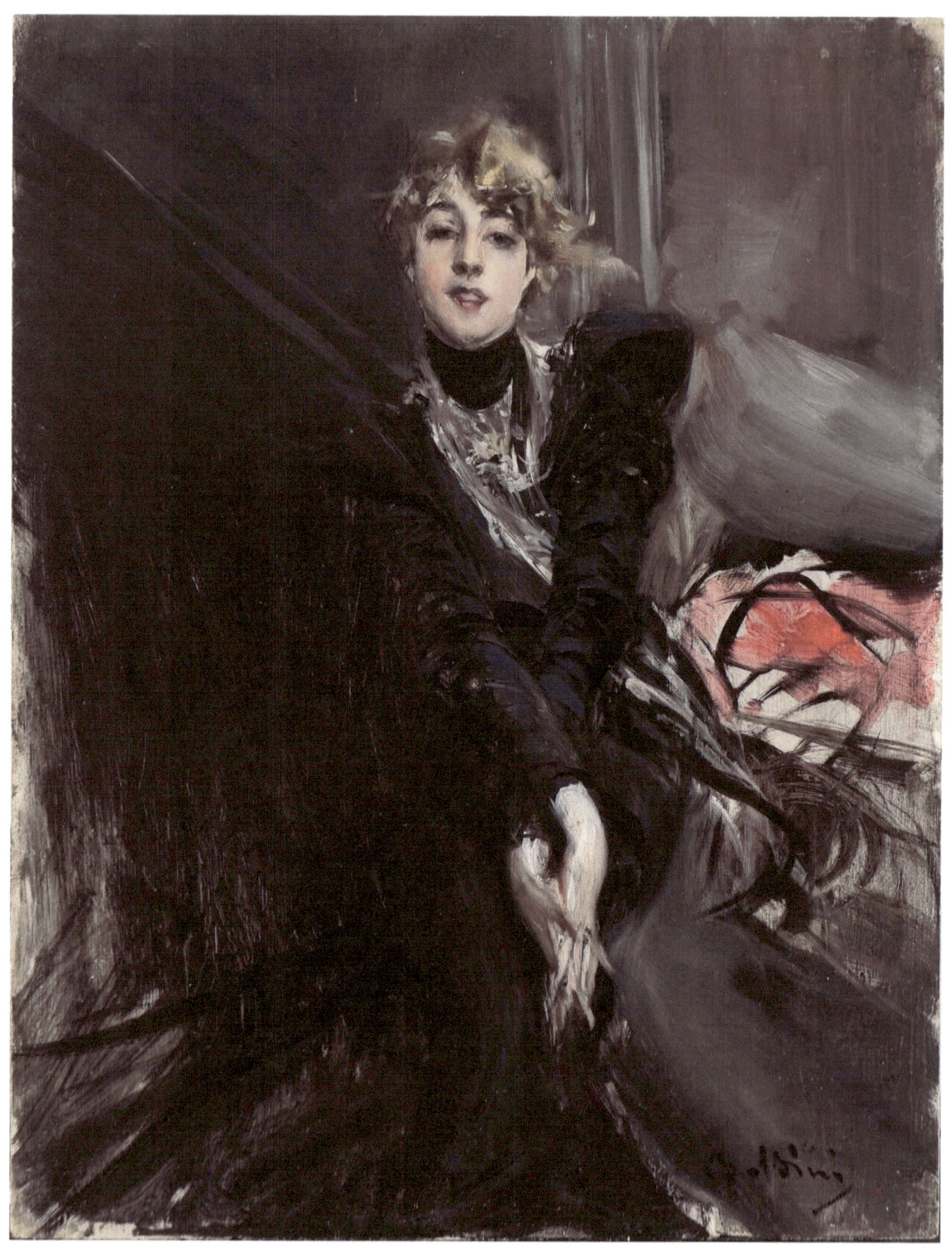

Portrait of the actress Jane Renouardt

1910, oil on panel, 35 x 27 cm, private collection

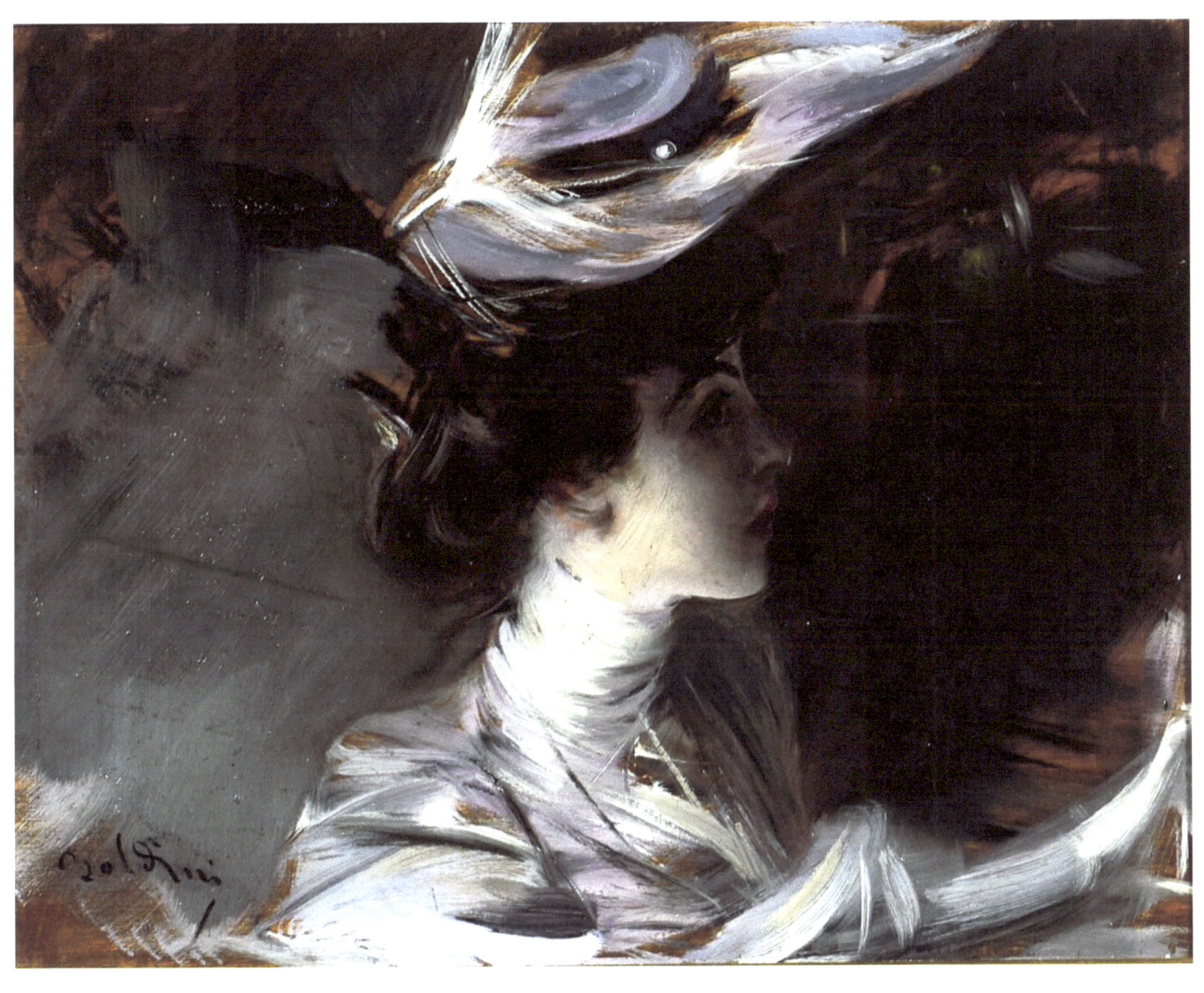

The new hat (Lina Cavalieri)

1900, oil on panel, 27 x 33 cm, private collection

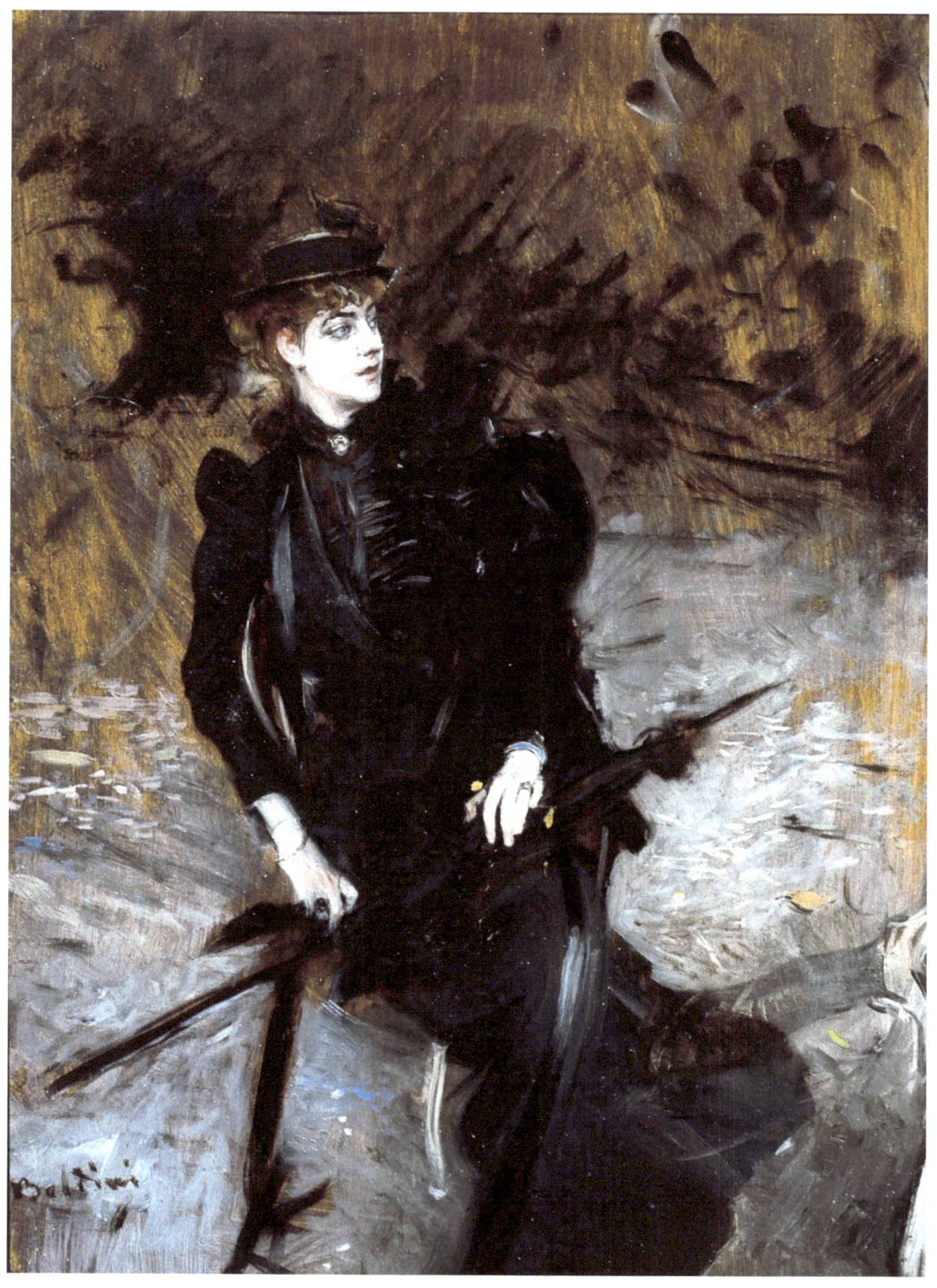

Portrait of Mrs. Henrietta Allegri

1894-1895, oil on canvas, 34.5 x 26.5 cm, private collection

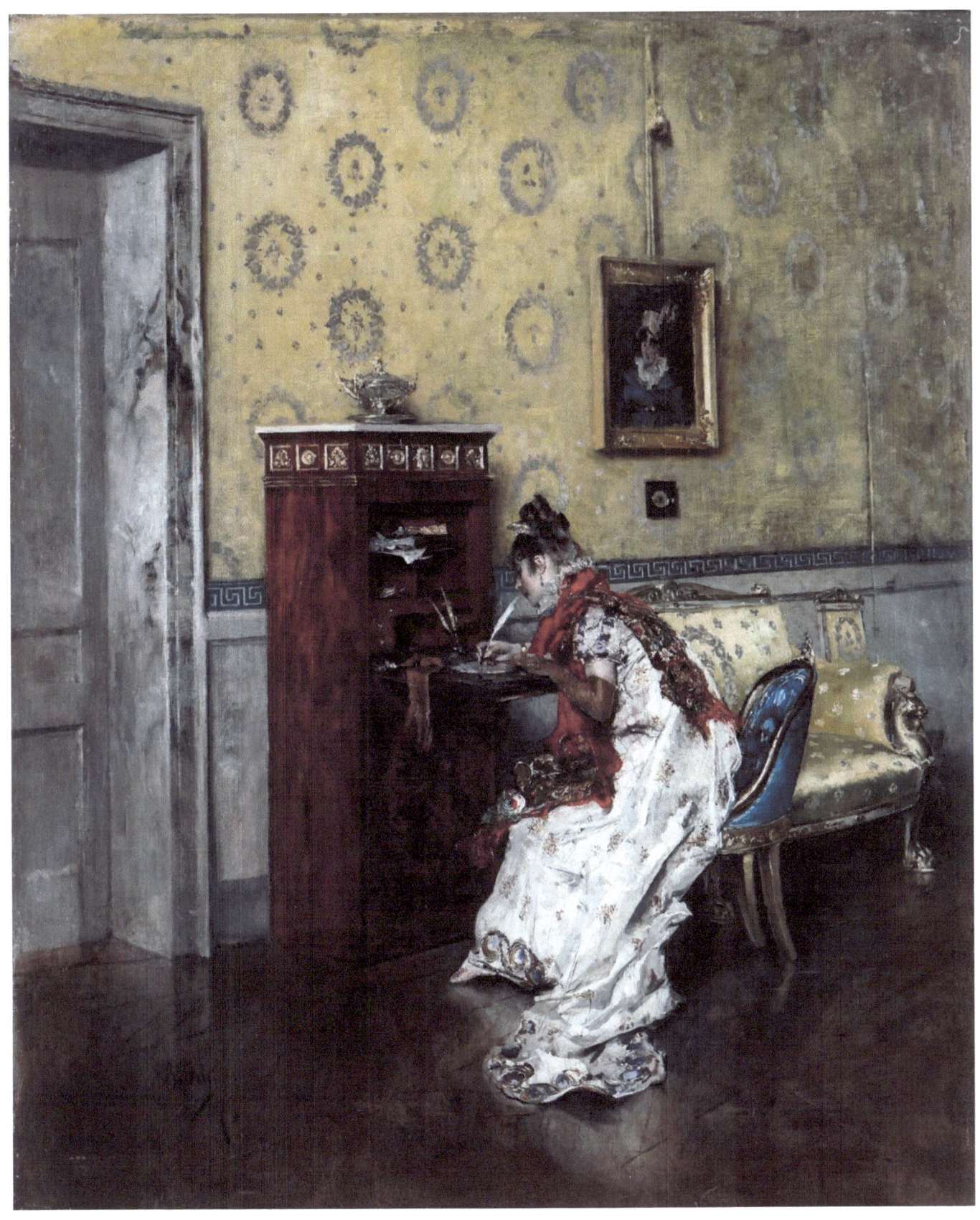

The letter (Young woman writing)

1873, Oil on canvas, 65 x 55 cm, private collection

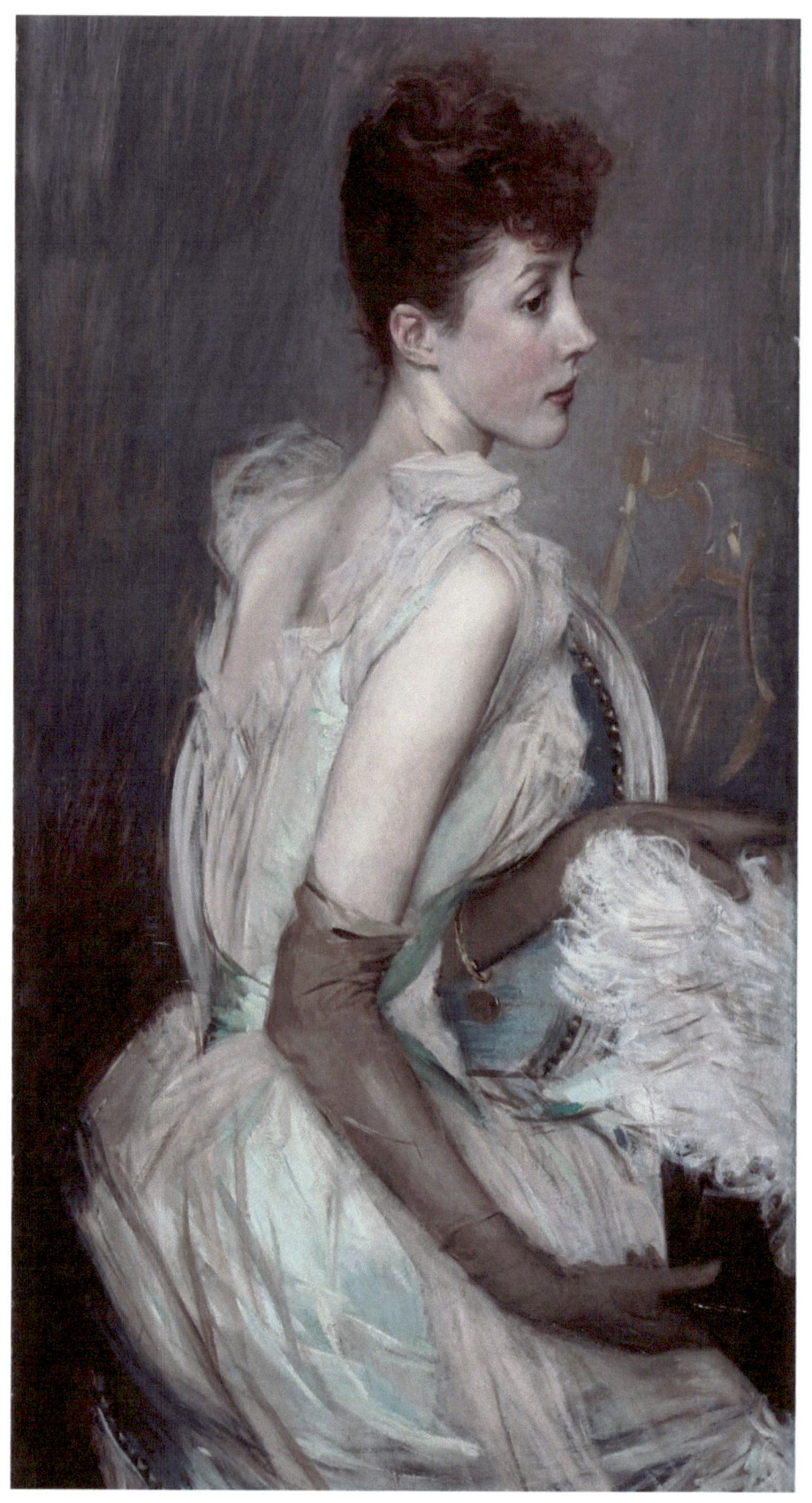

Portrait of the Countess De Leusse, born Berthier

1890, Oil on canvas, 170 x 59 cm, private collection

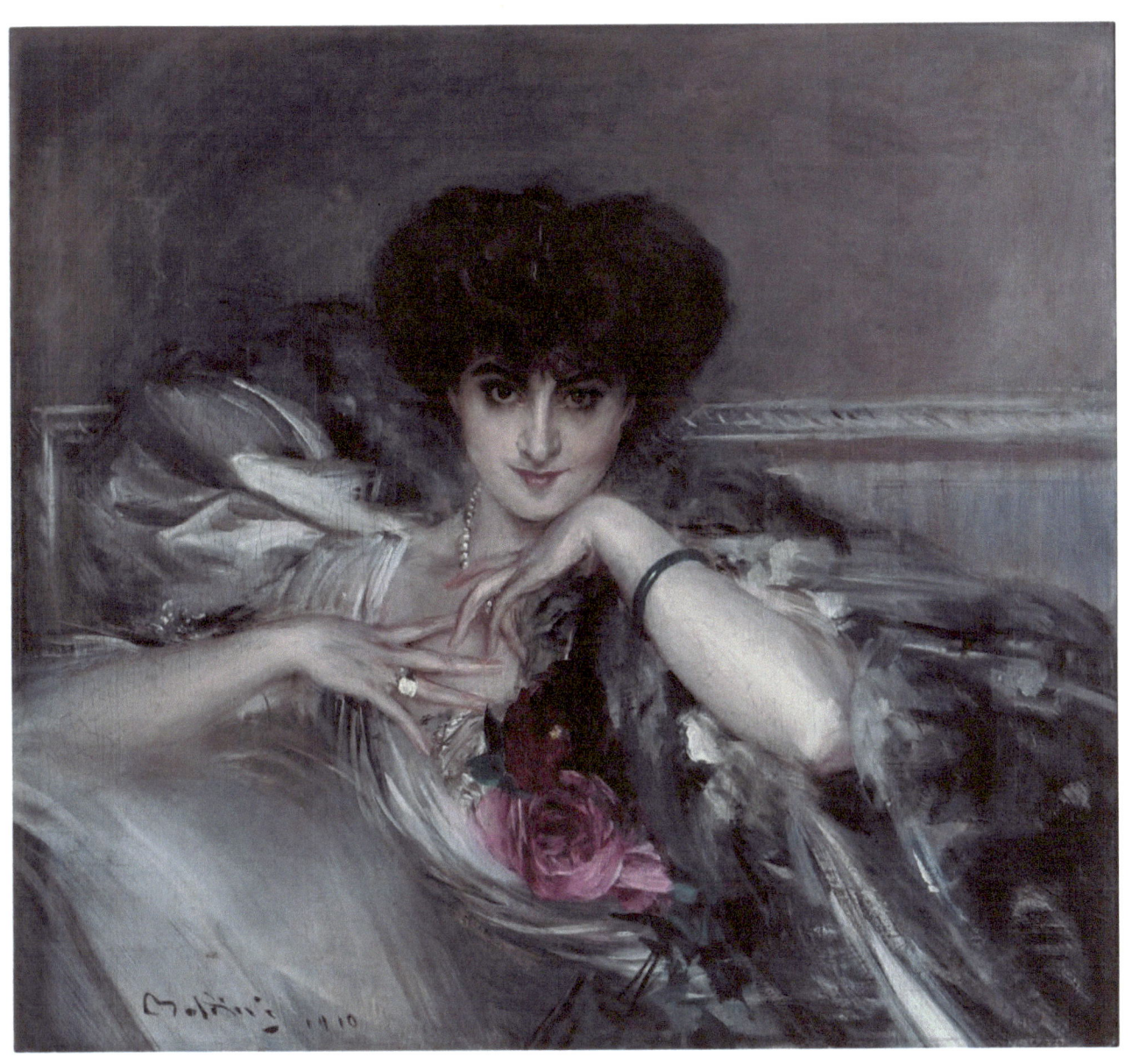

Portrait of Princess Radziwill

1910, Oil on canvas, 82,5x91 cm, Private collection

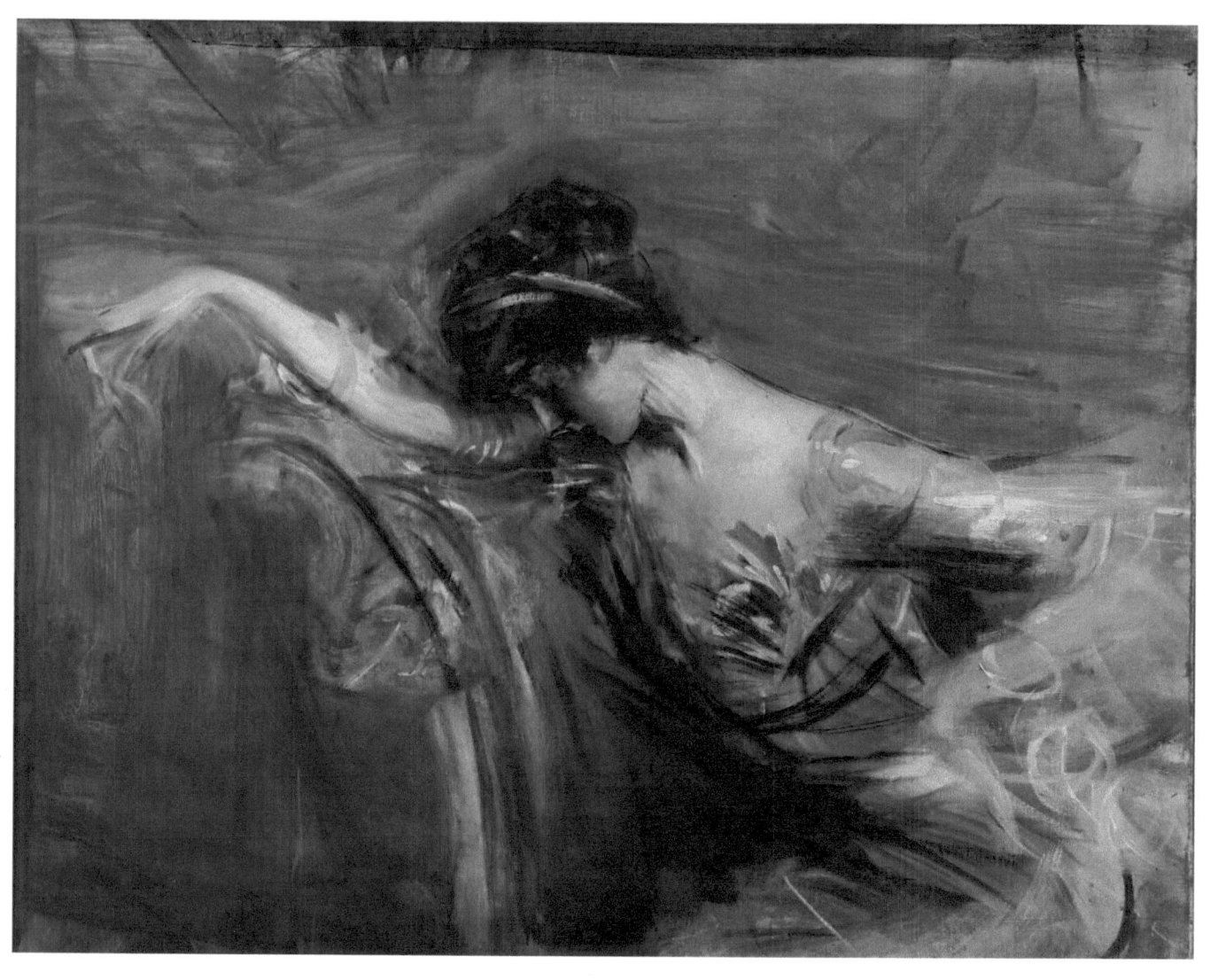

Mademoiselle Laure

1910, Oil on canvas, 46 x 66 cm, private collection

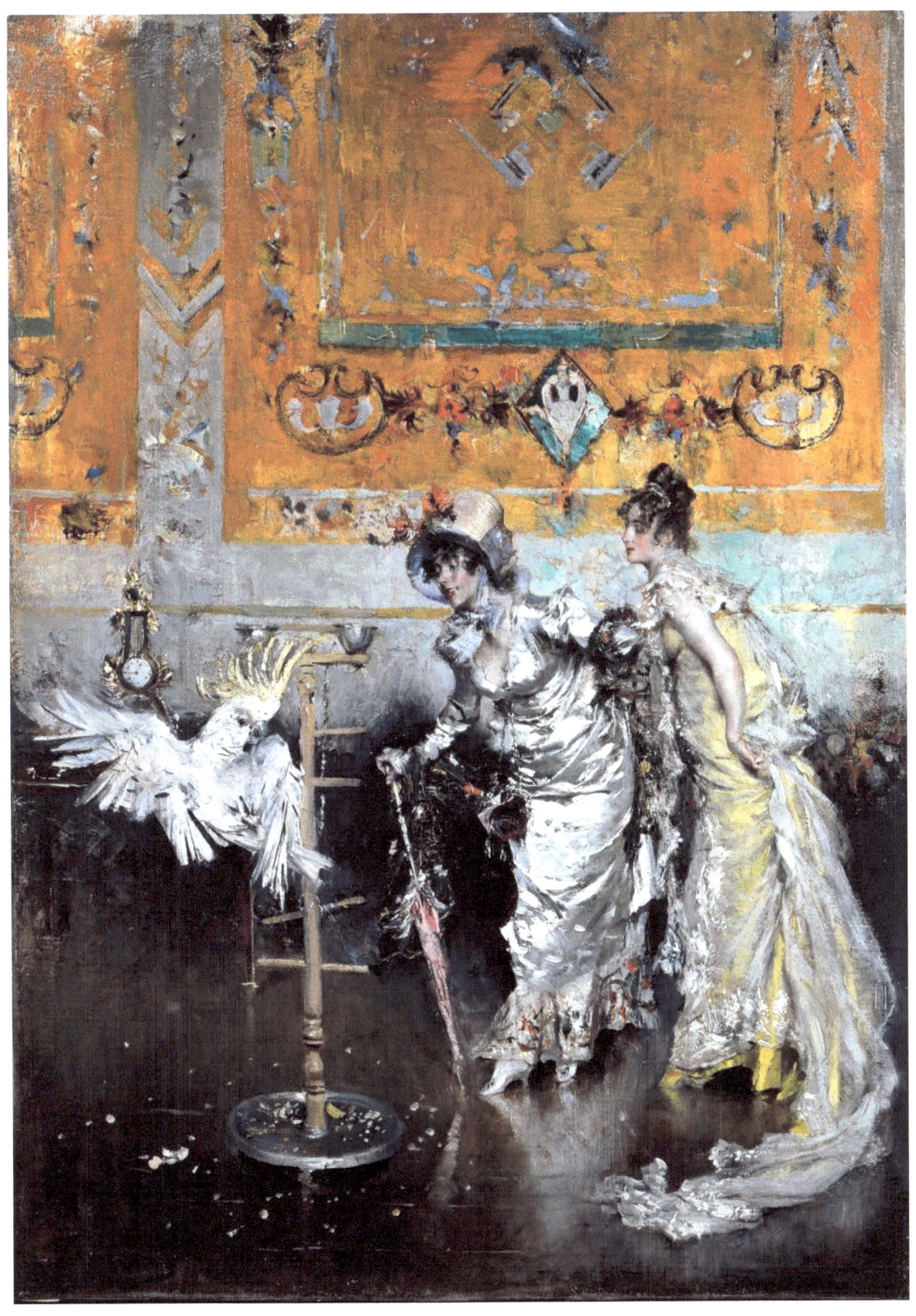

Two ladies with parrot (Taquinant the perrequet)

1872, Private collection

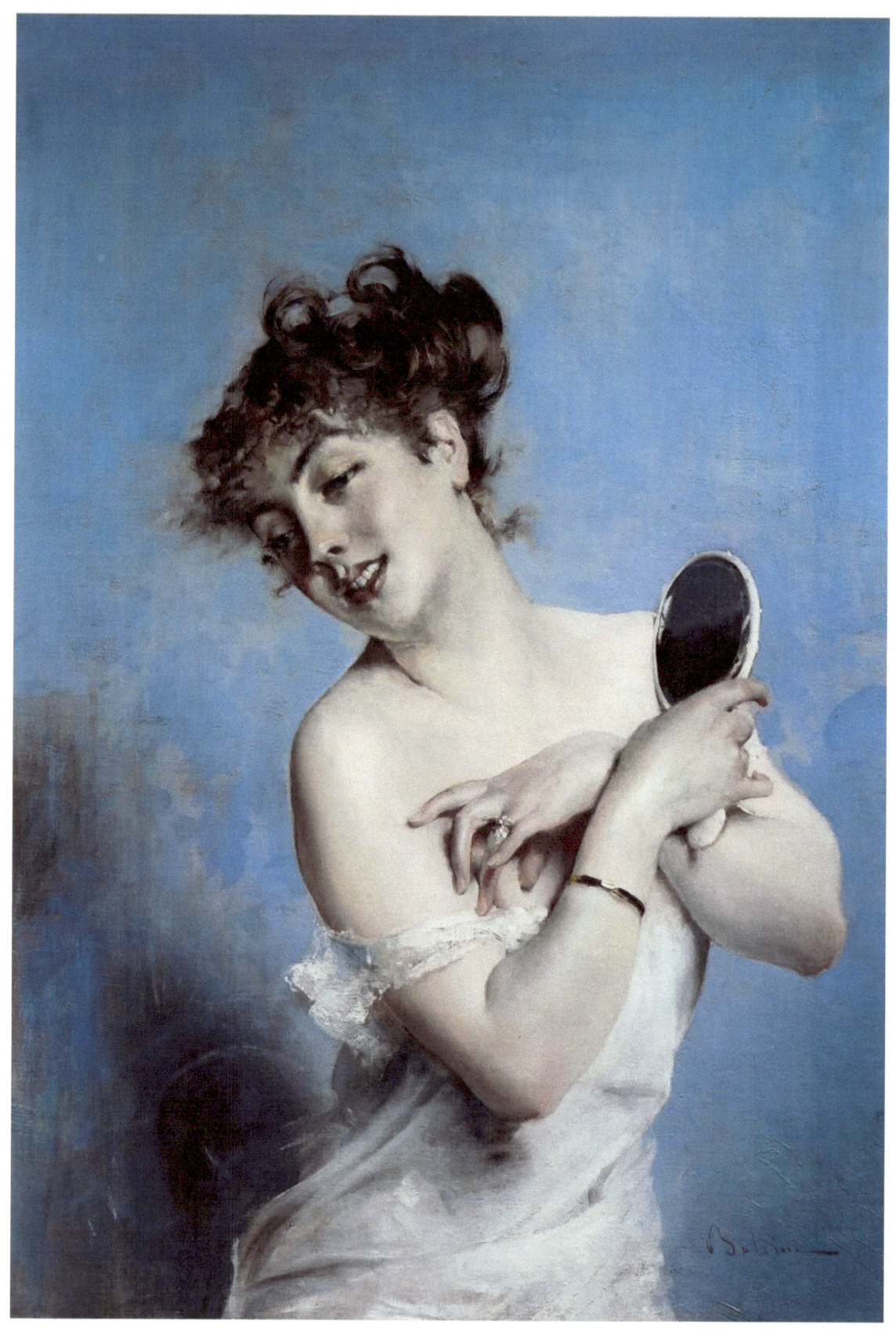

Young in Girl with mirror (The Dressing)

1880, Oil on canvas, 81x60 cm, Private collection

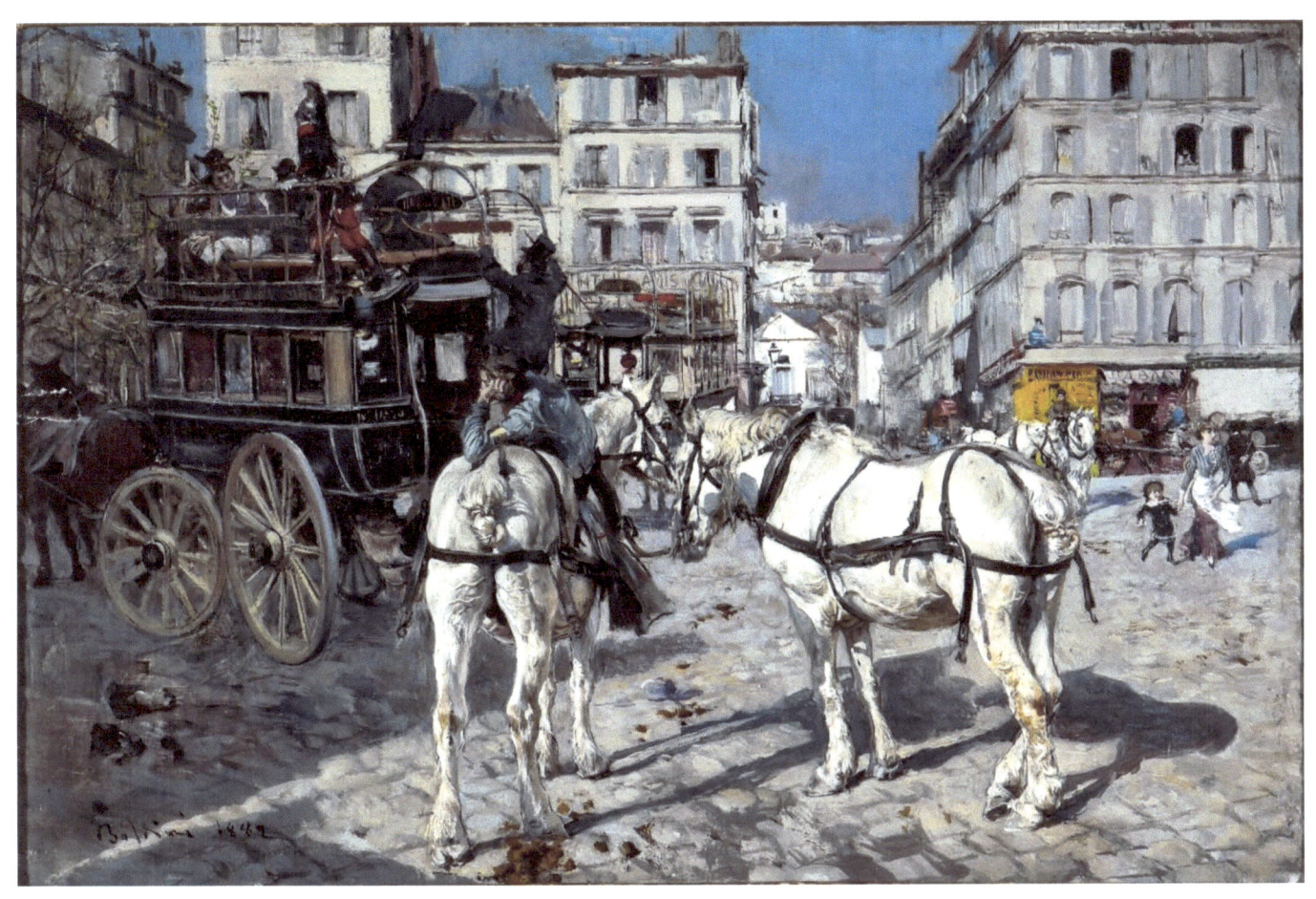

Omnibus in Place Pigalle

1882, oil on canvas, private collection

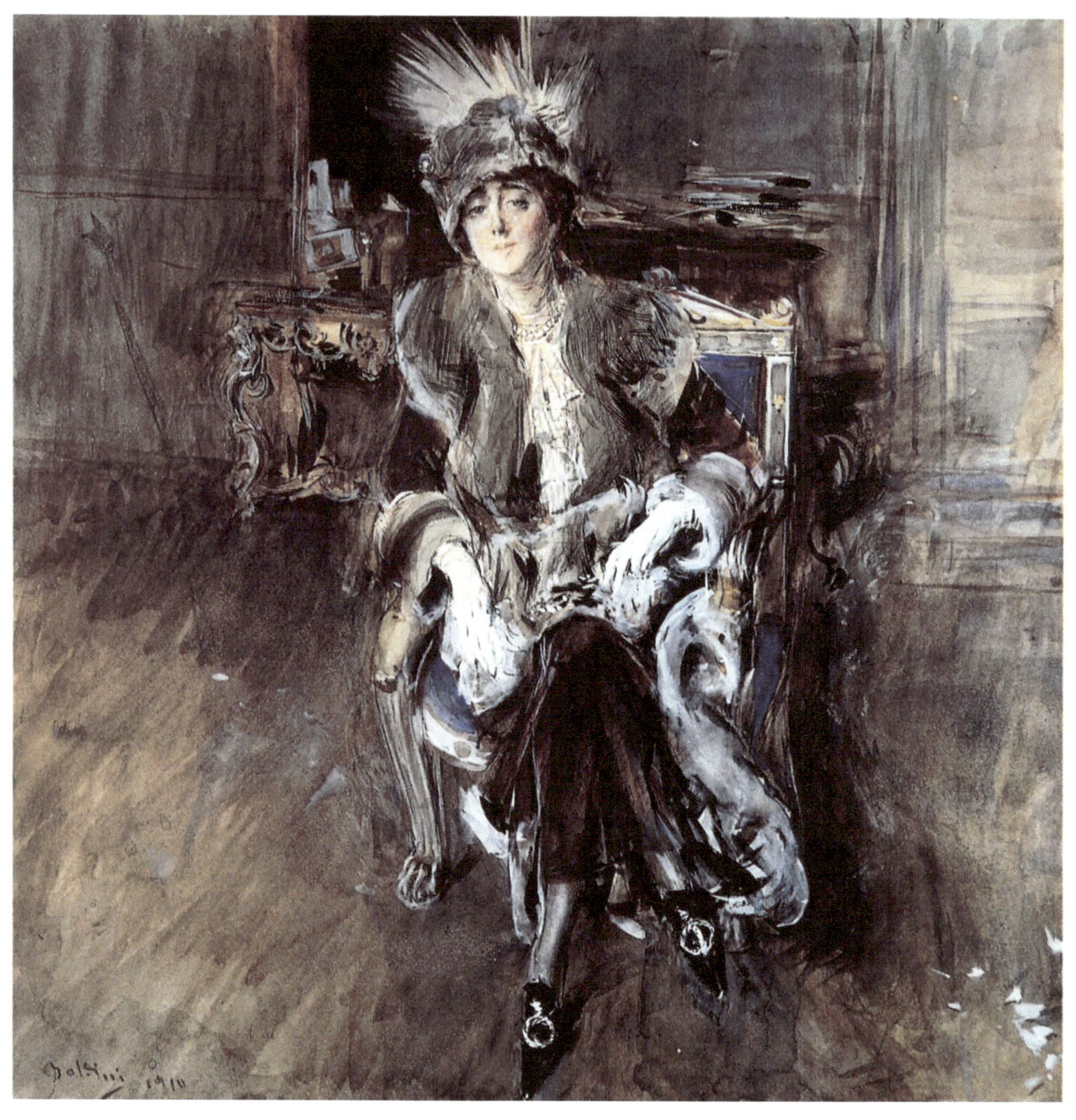

Portrait of Madame Lacroix

1910, watercolor on paper, 490x490 mm, Private collection

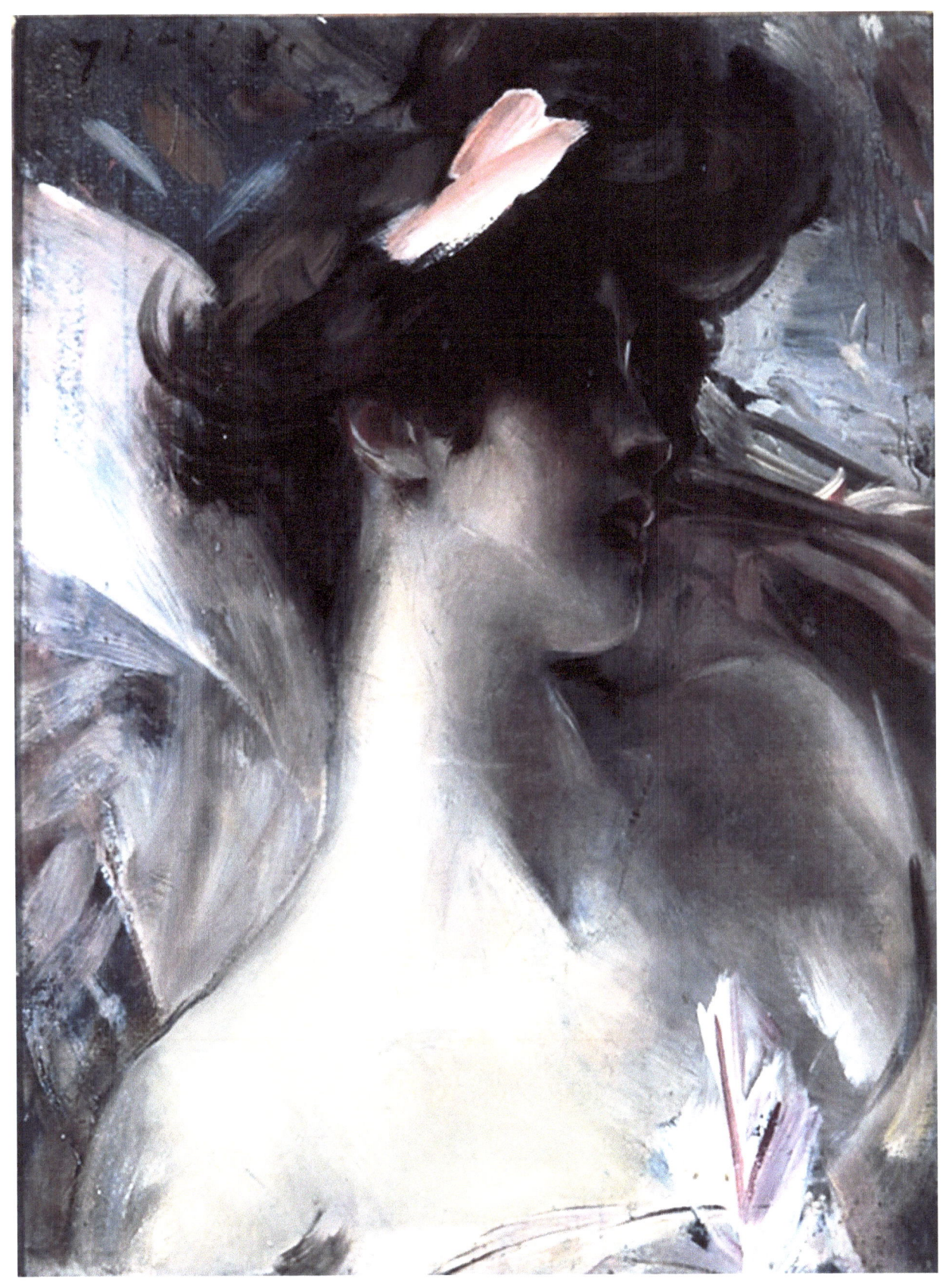

Head of a young brunette on a pink background,

1912, 50x38 cm, Private collection

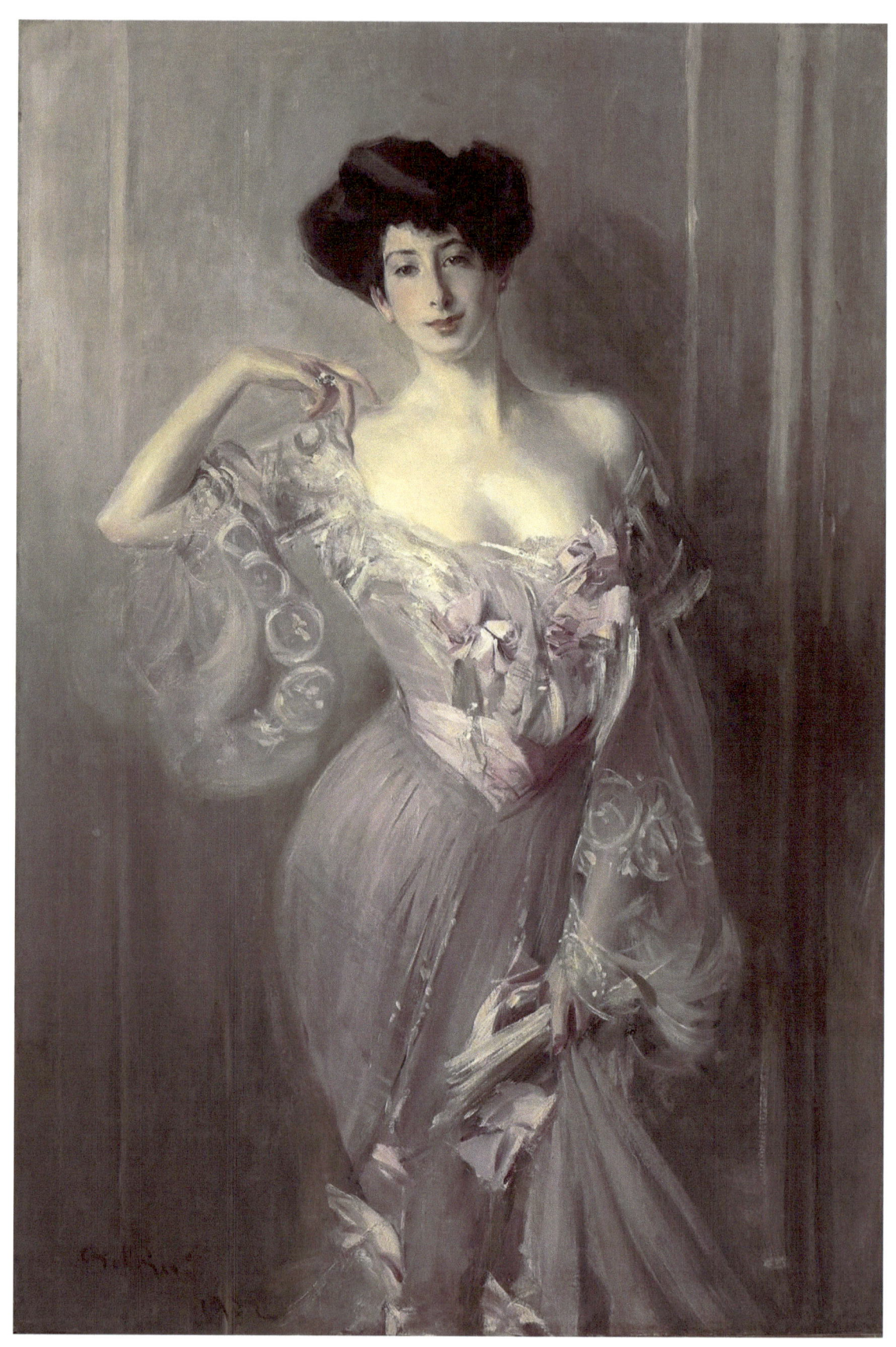

Steisy Lineth Mercado

Oil on canvas

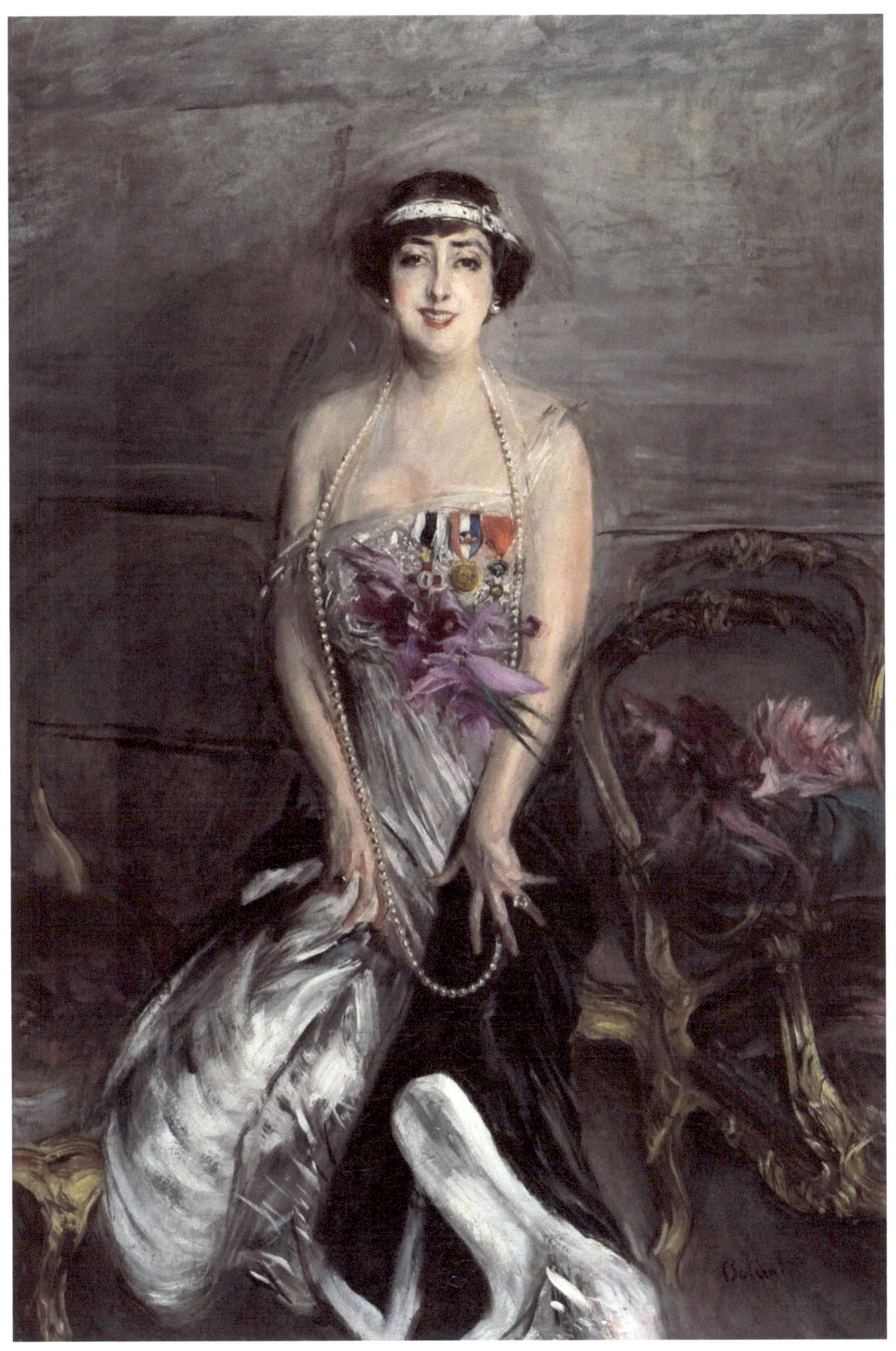

Madame Michelham

Oil on canvas

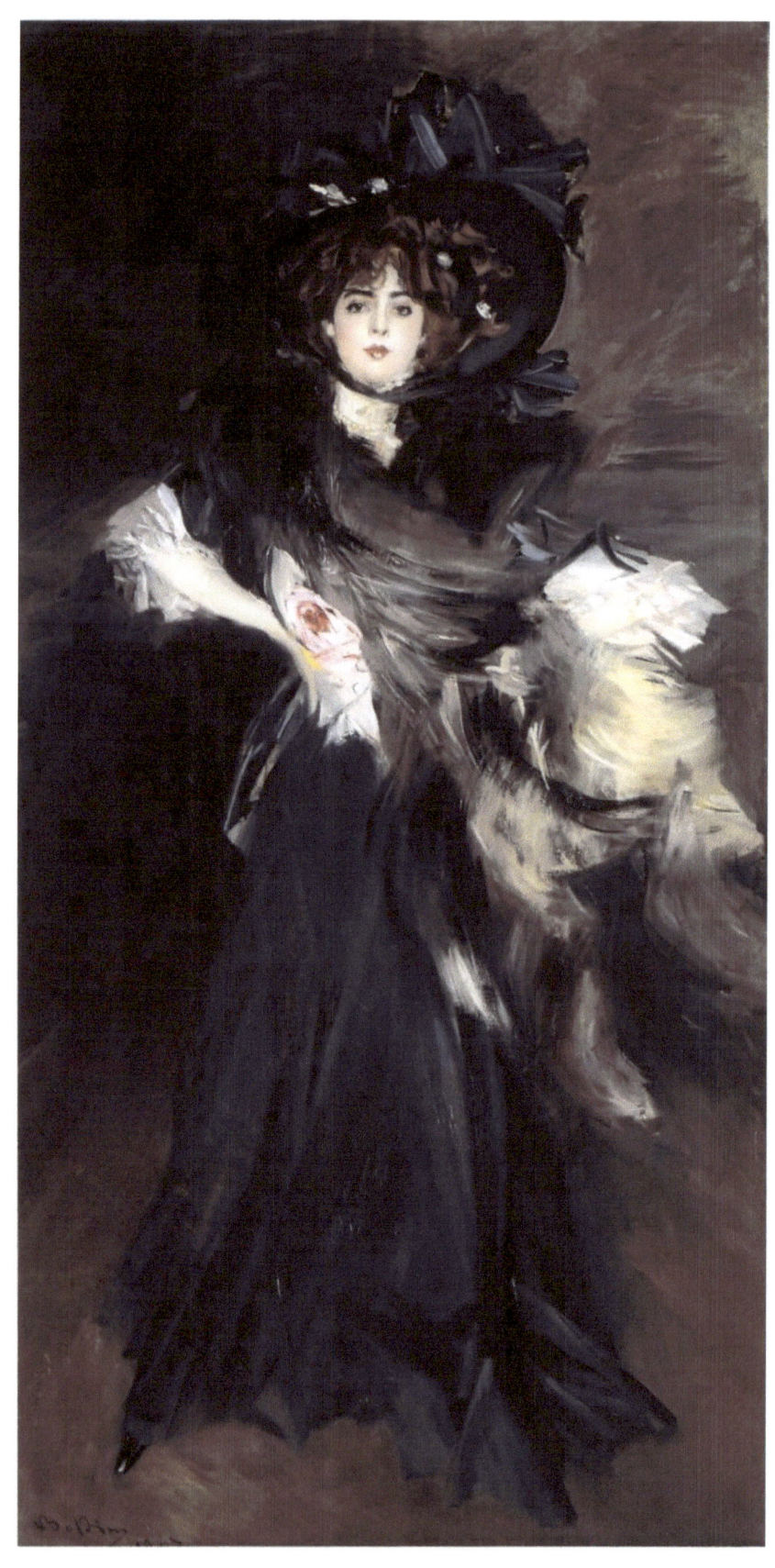

Mlle Lantelme

1907, Oil on canvas

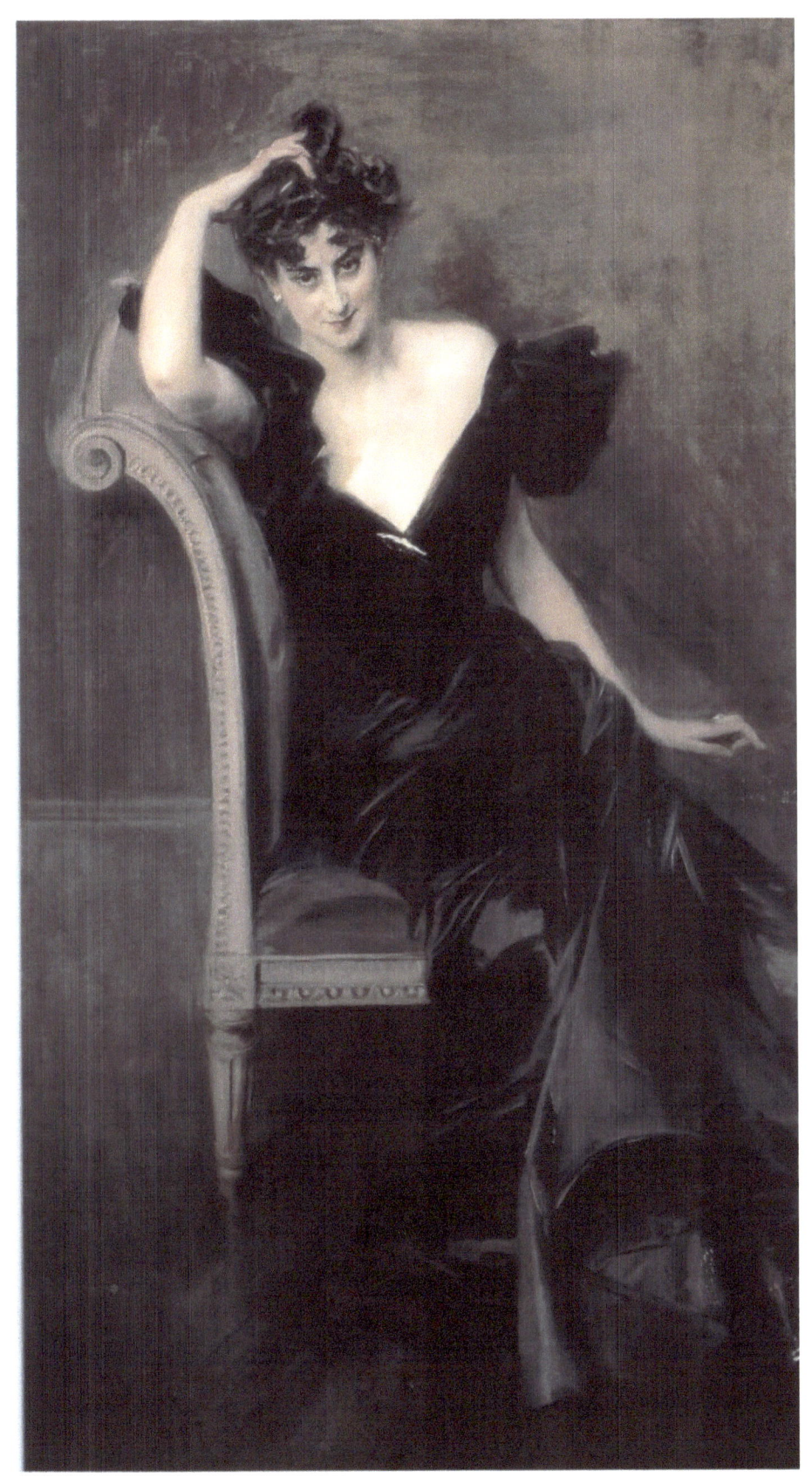

M-me Veil Picard

1897, Oil on canvas

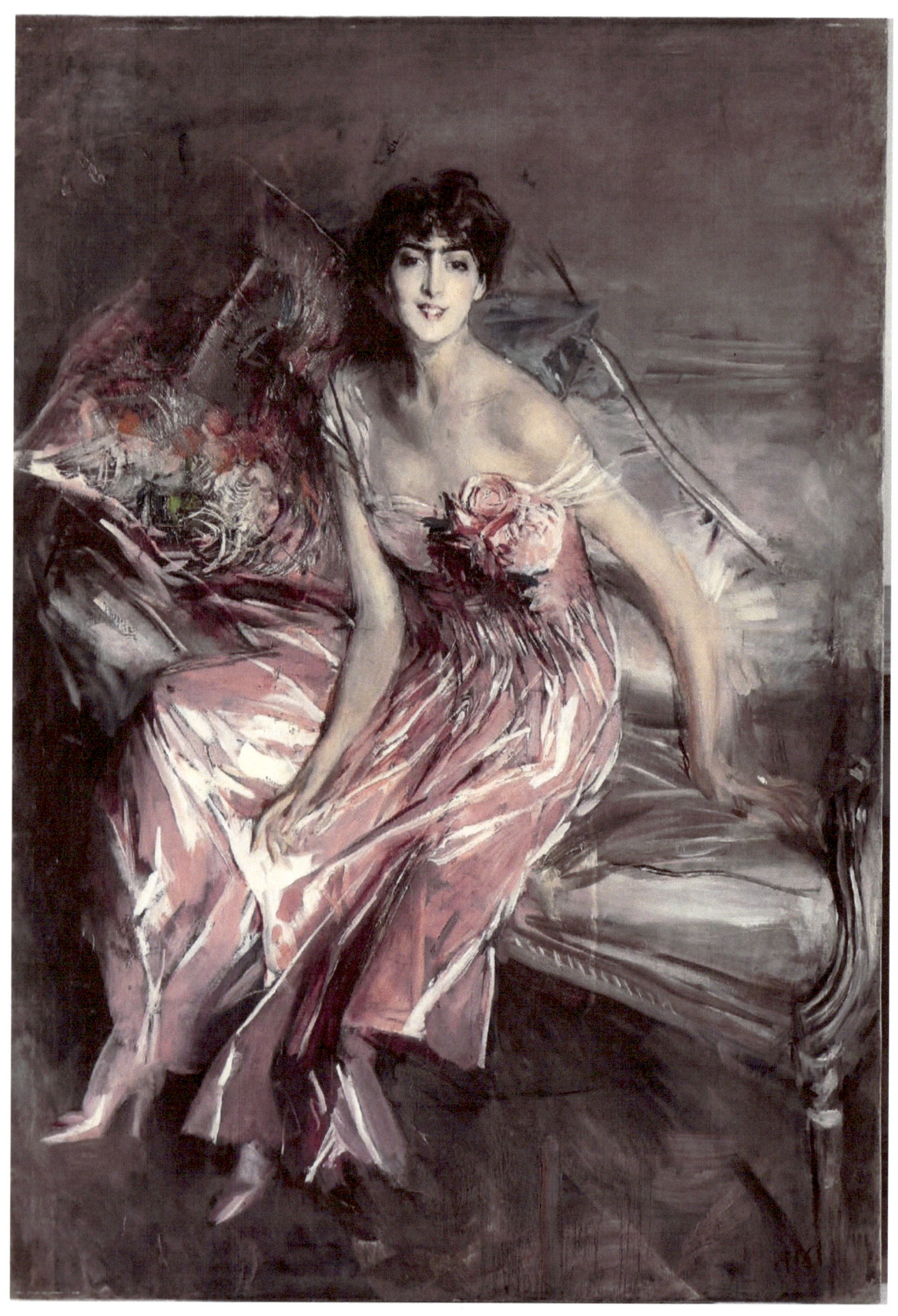

The lady in pink

1916, Oil on canvas

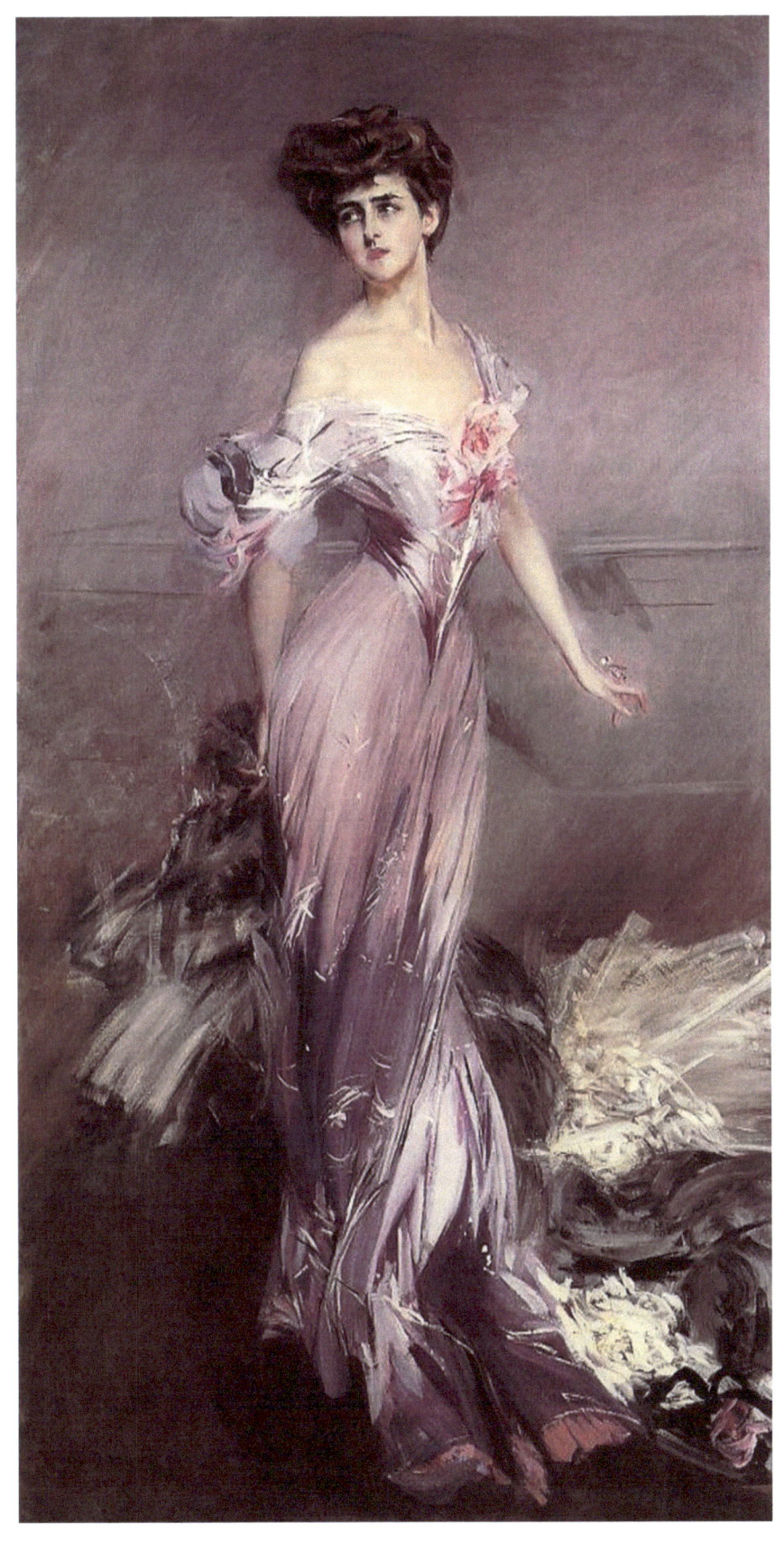

Portrait of Mrs. Howard-Johnston (Dolly Baird of Bunbarton)

1906, oil on canvas, Private collection

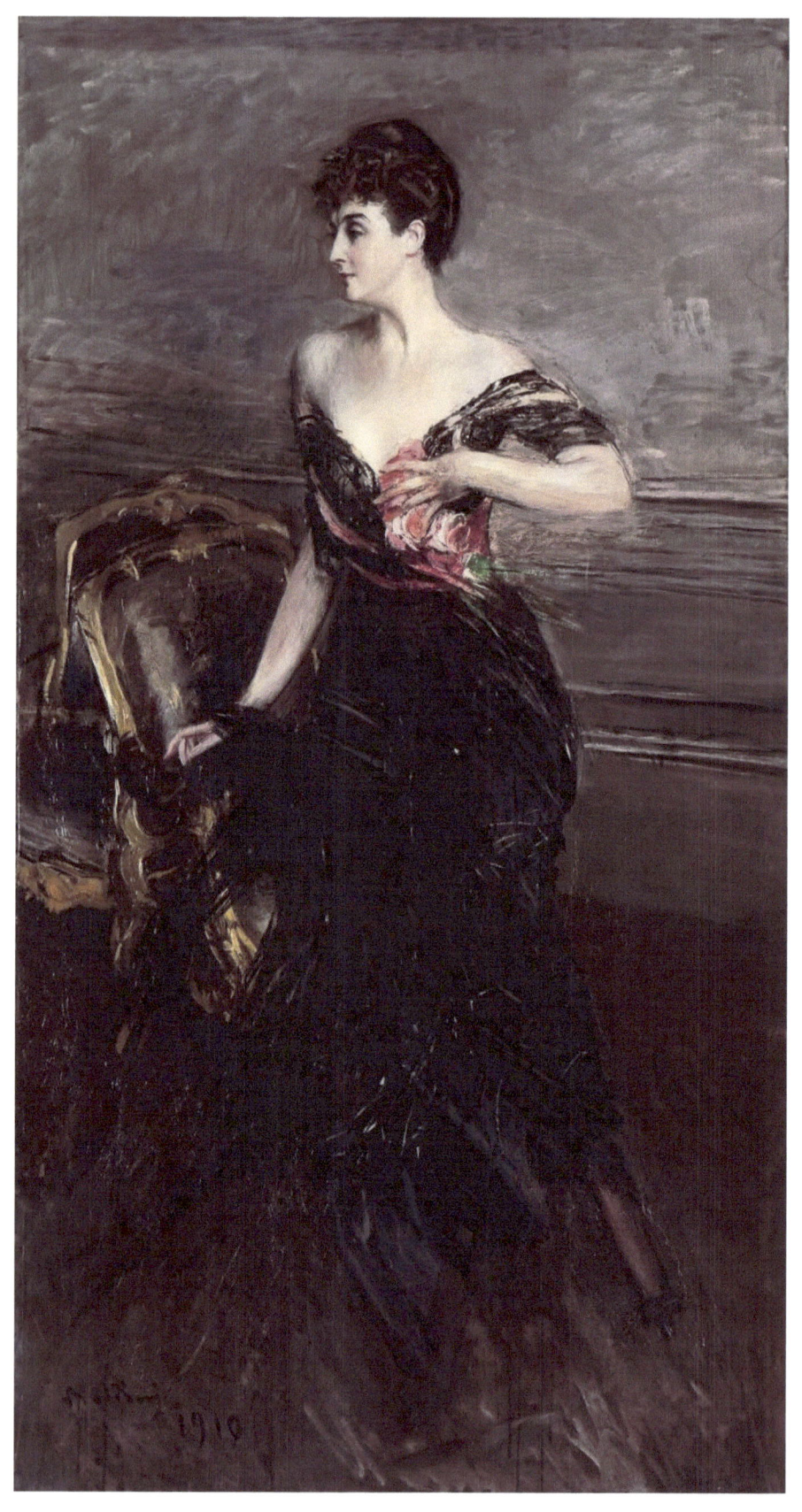

Cécile Murat Ney d'Elchingen

Oil on canvas

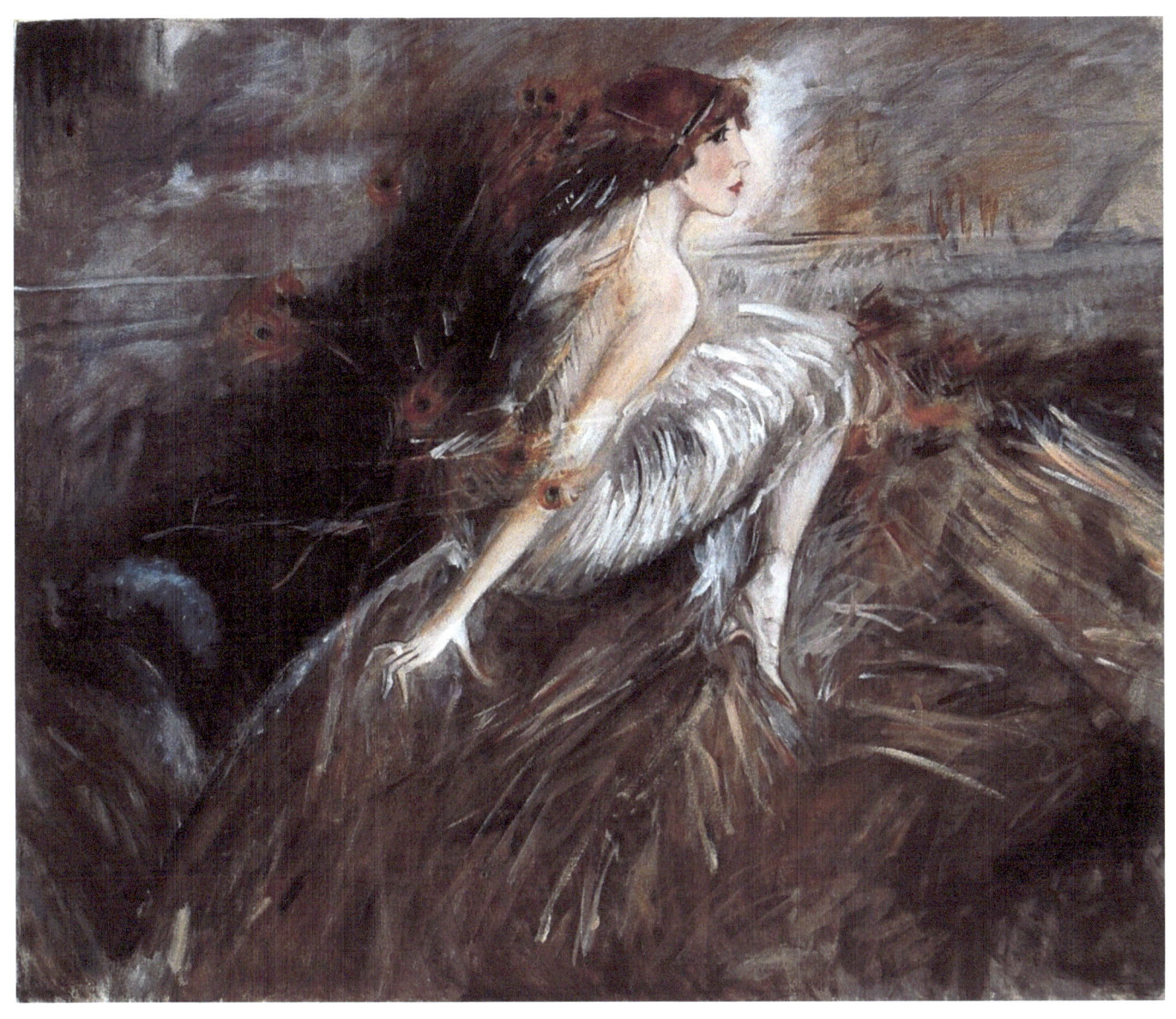

Marchesa Casati Luigia With Peacock Feathers

Oil on canvas

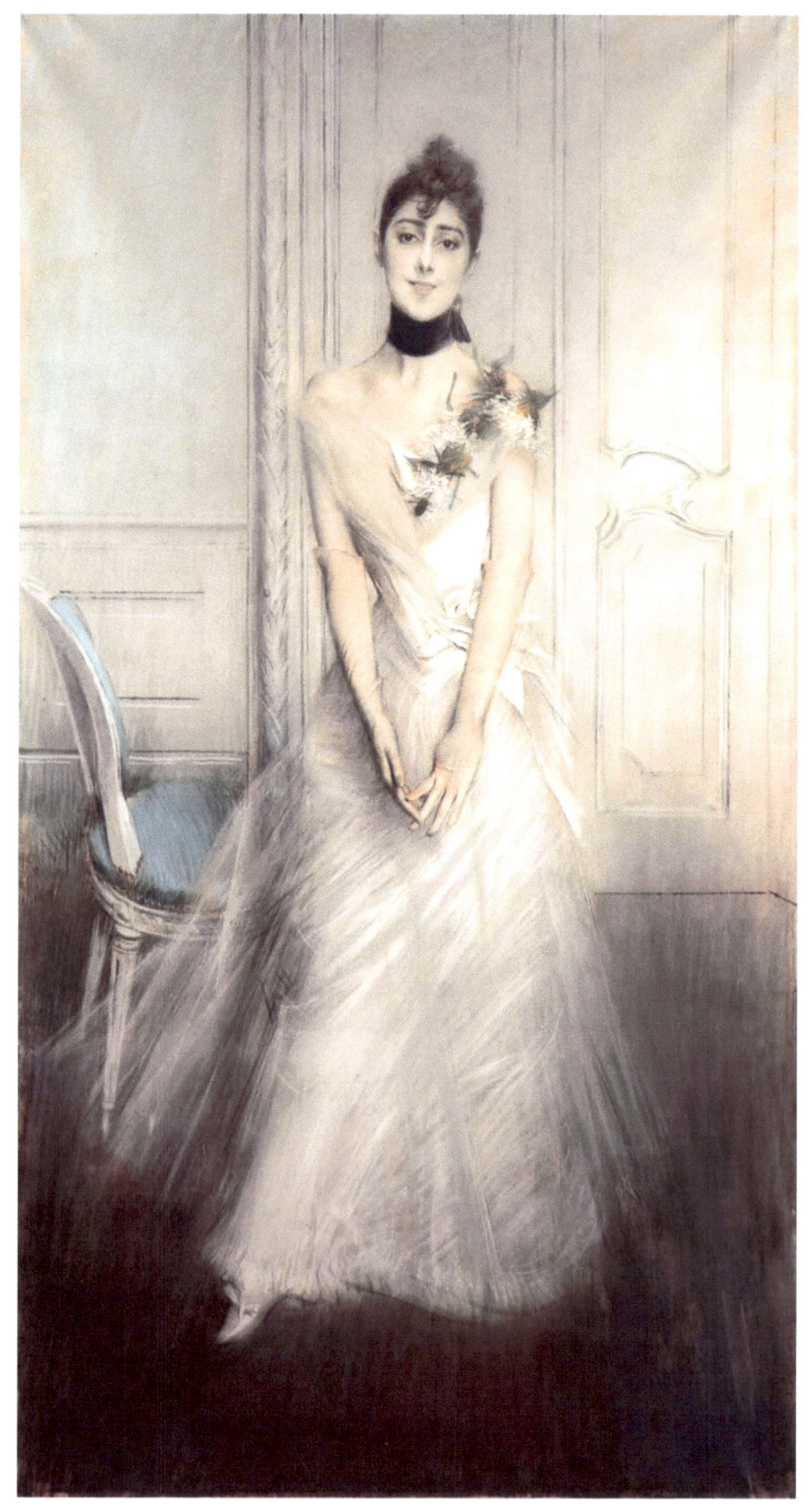

Portrait of Emiliana Concha de Ossa

Oil on canvas

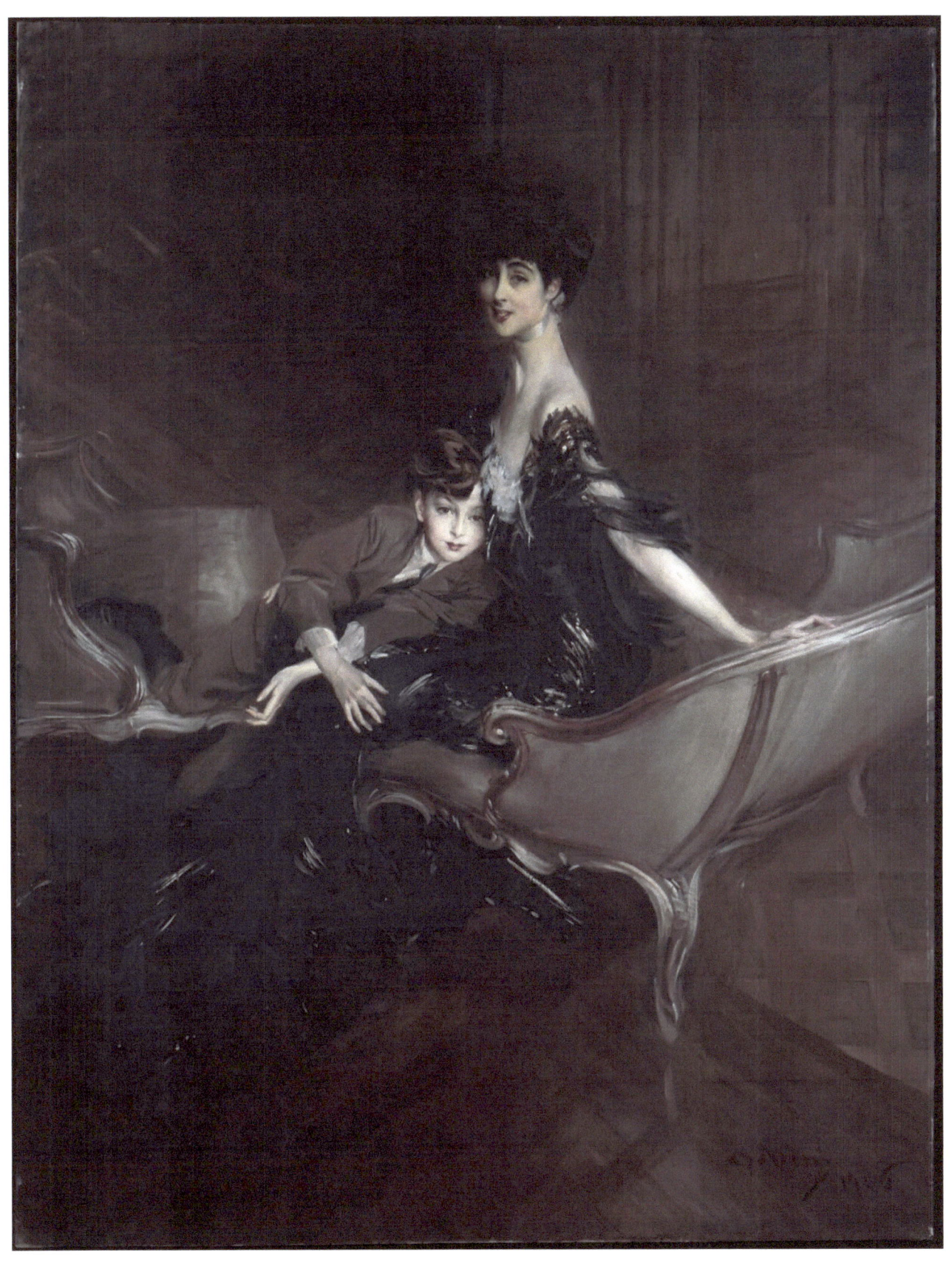

Consuelo Vanderbilt and her son Ivor

1906, Oil on canvas

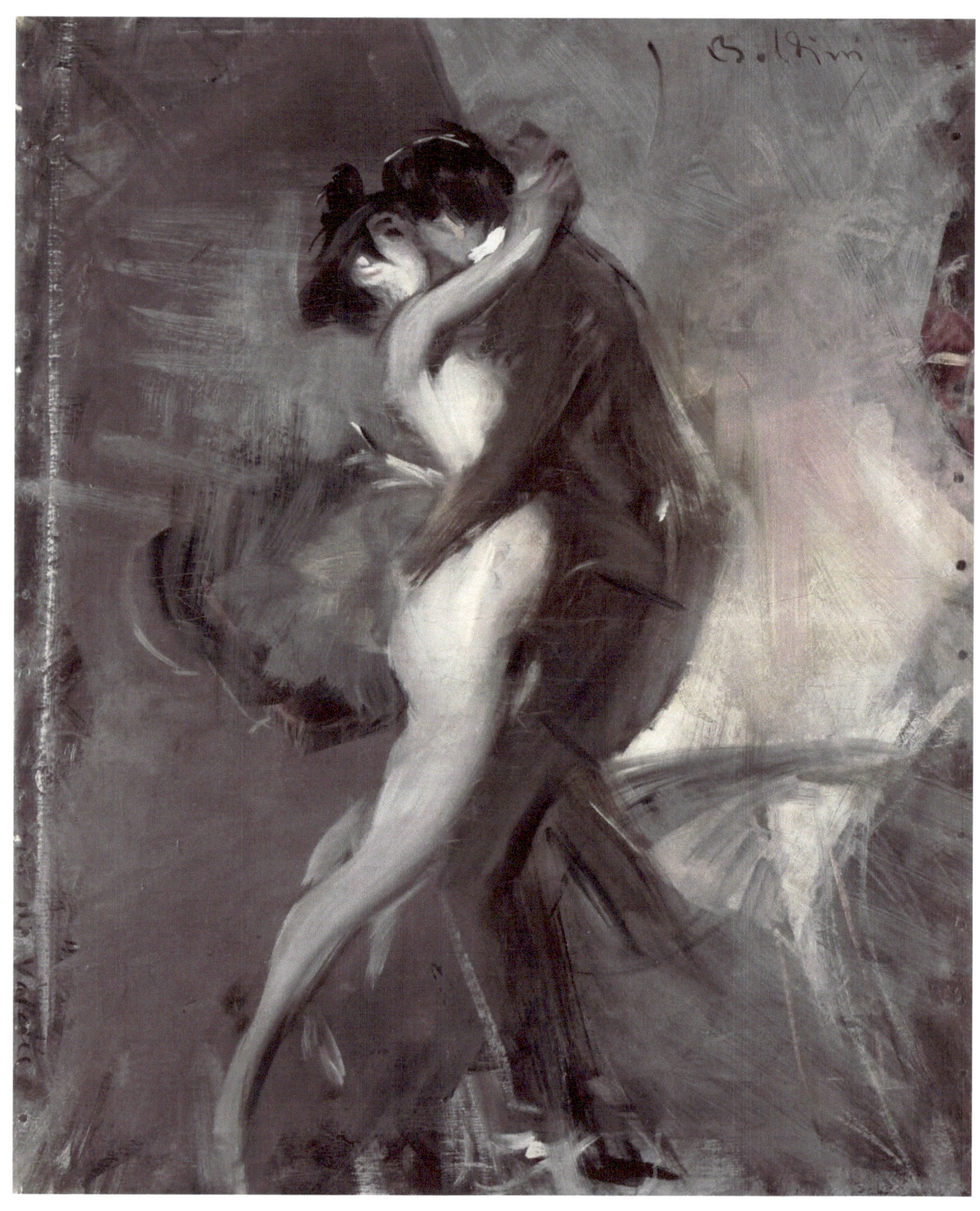

The Couple

1905, Oil on canvas

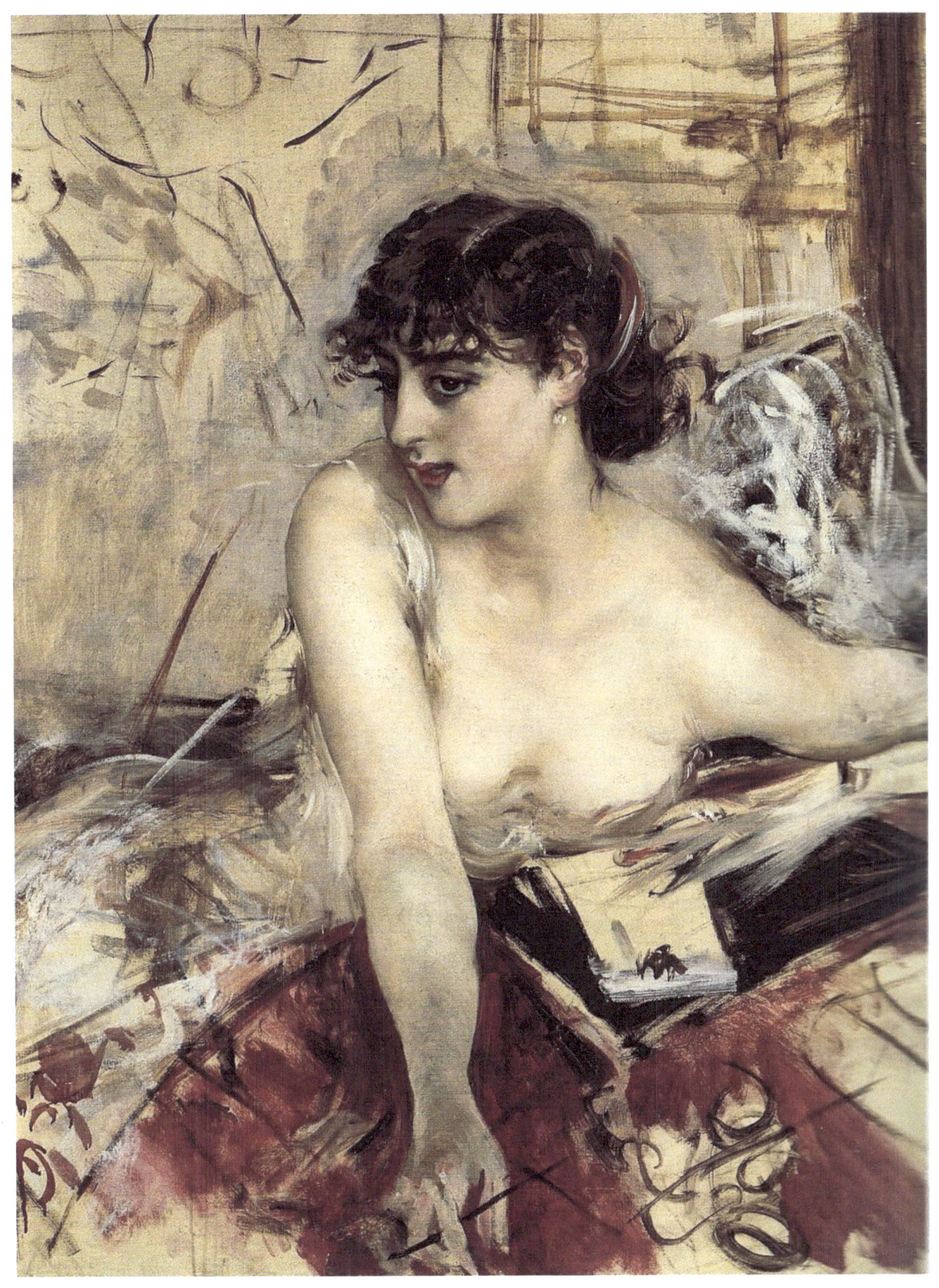

The morning letter

Oil on canvas

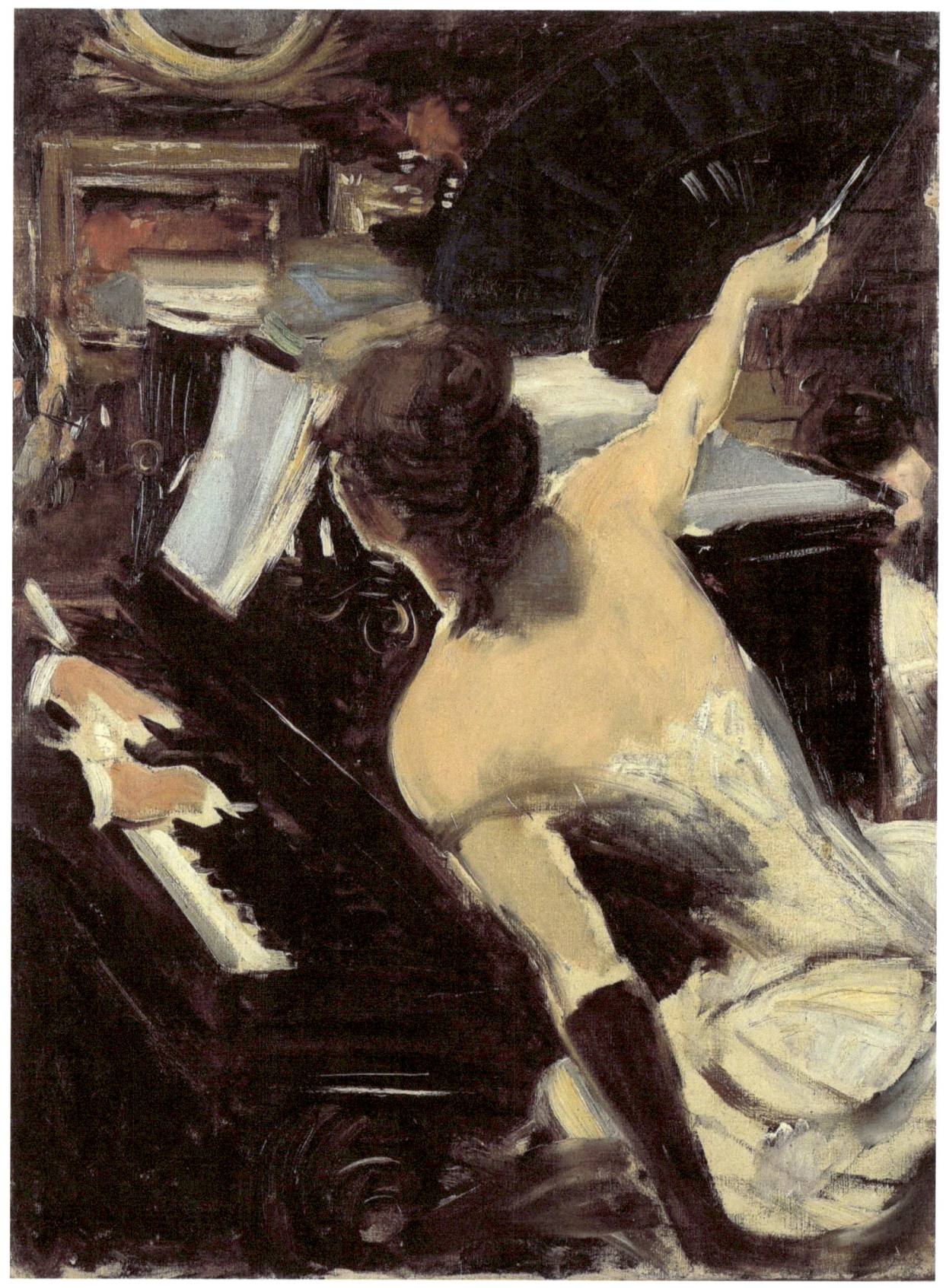

The Singer

1884, Oil on canvas, 61 x 46 cm

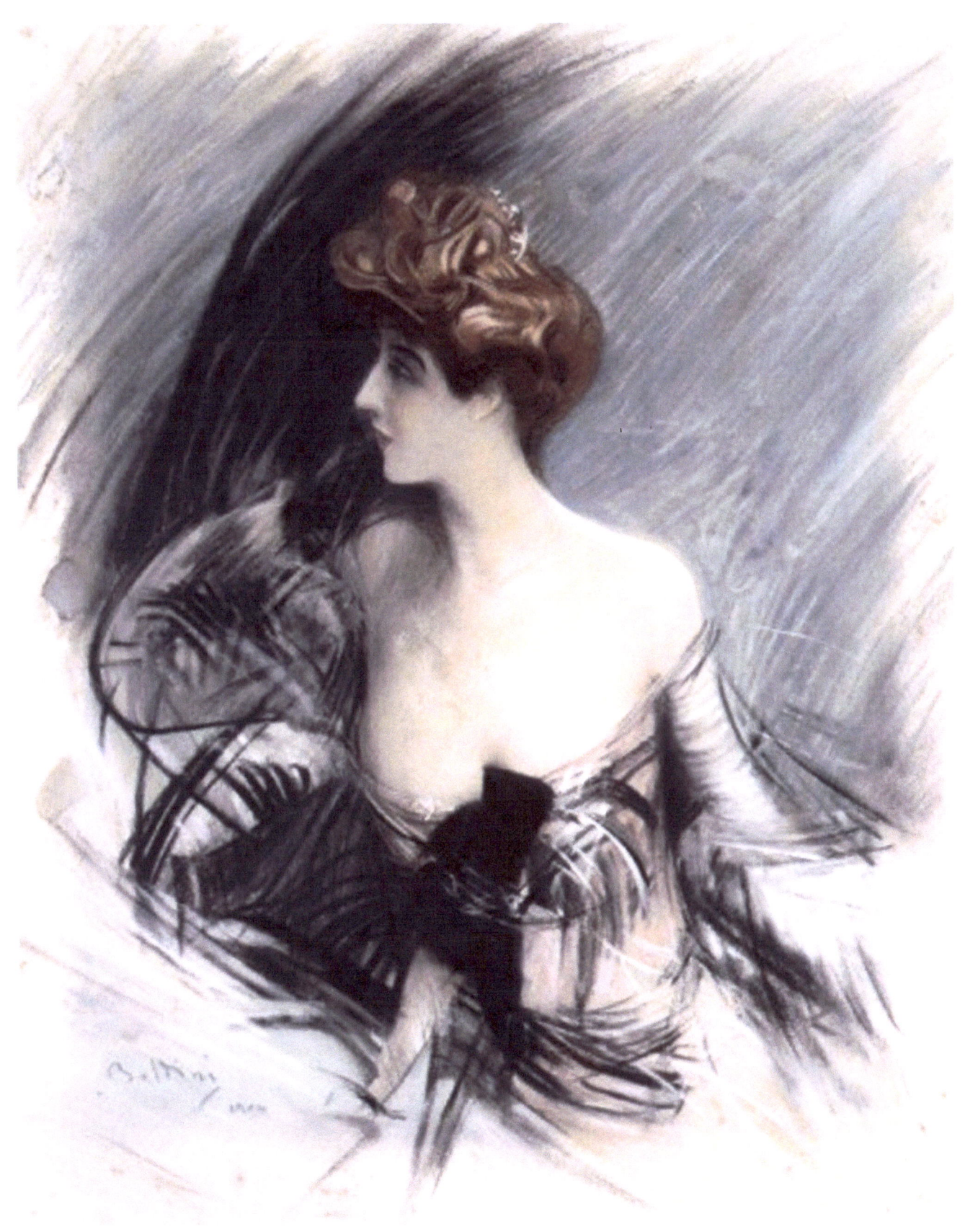

Portrait of Sarah Bernhardt

1880

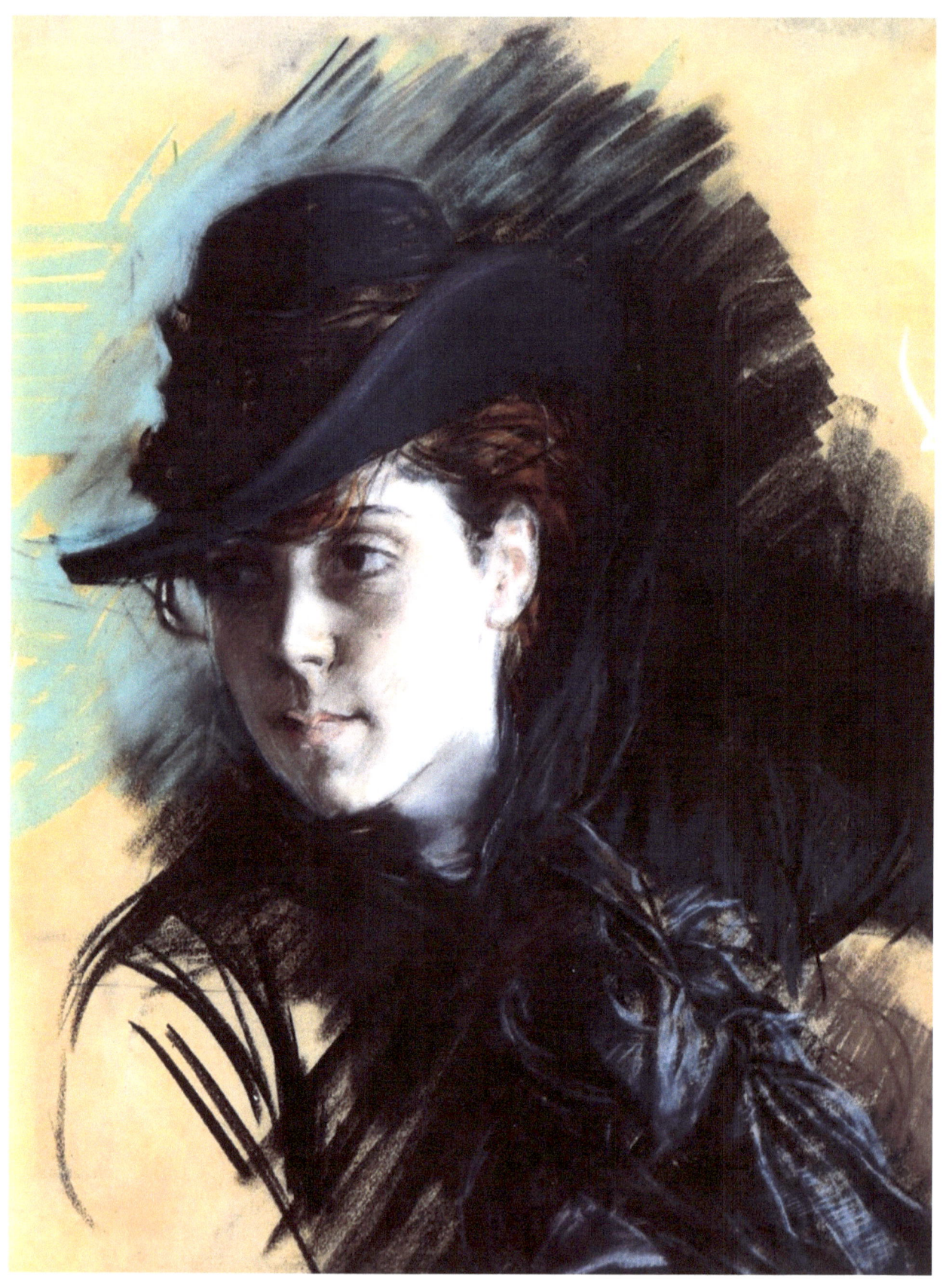

Girl In A Black Hat

Oil on canvas

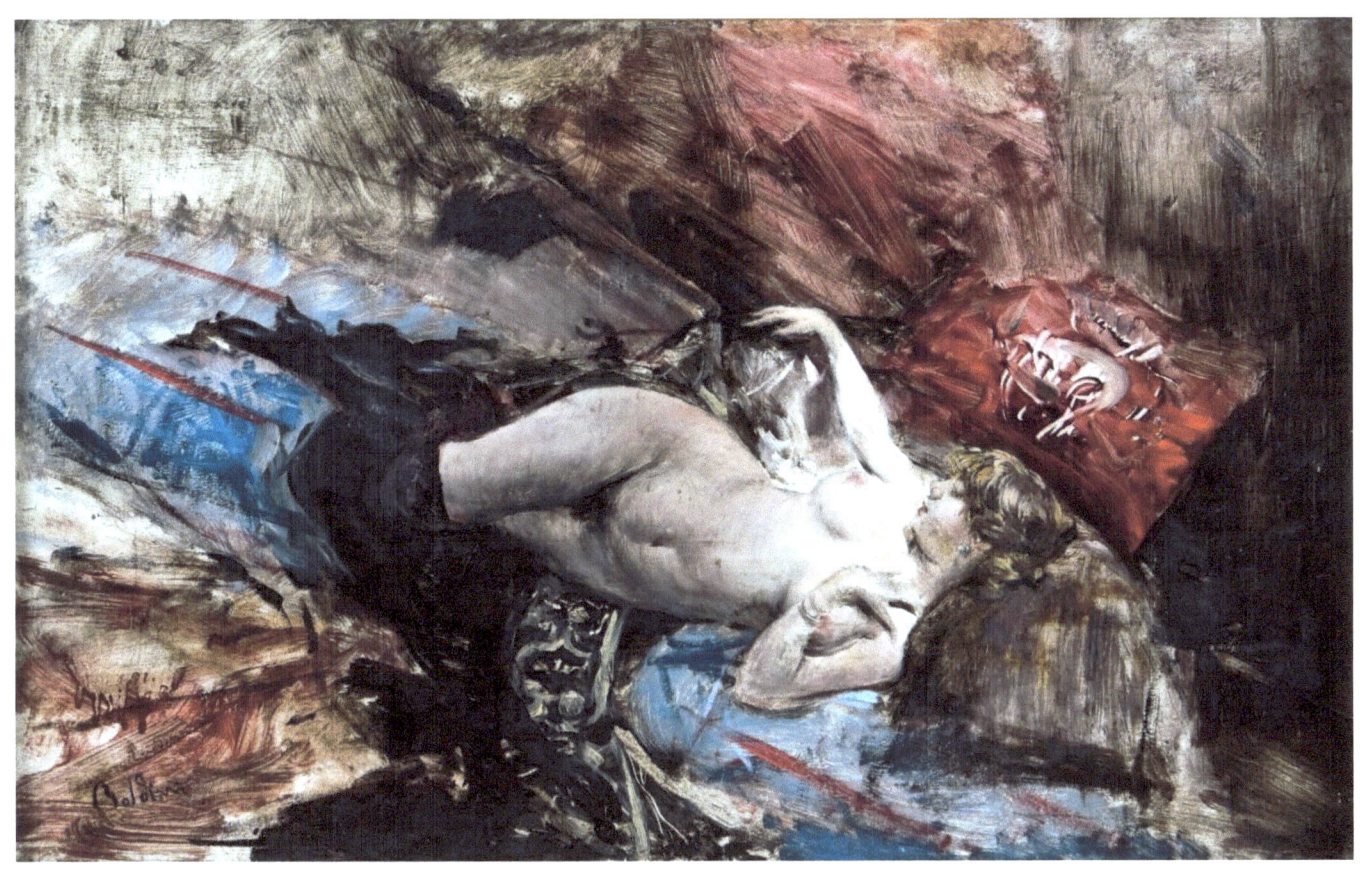

Nude woman with black stockings

1885, Oil on canvas

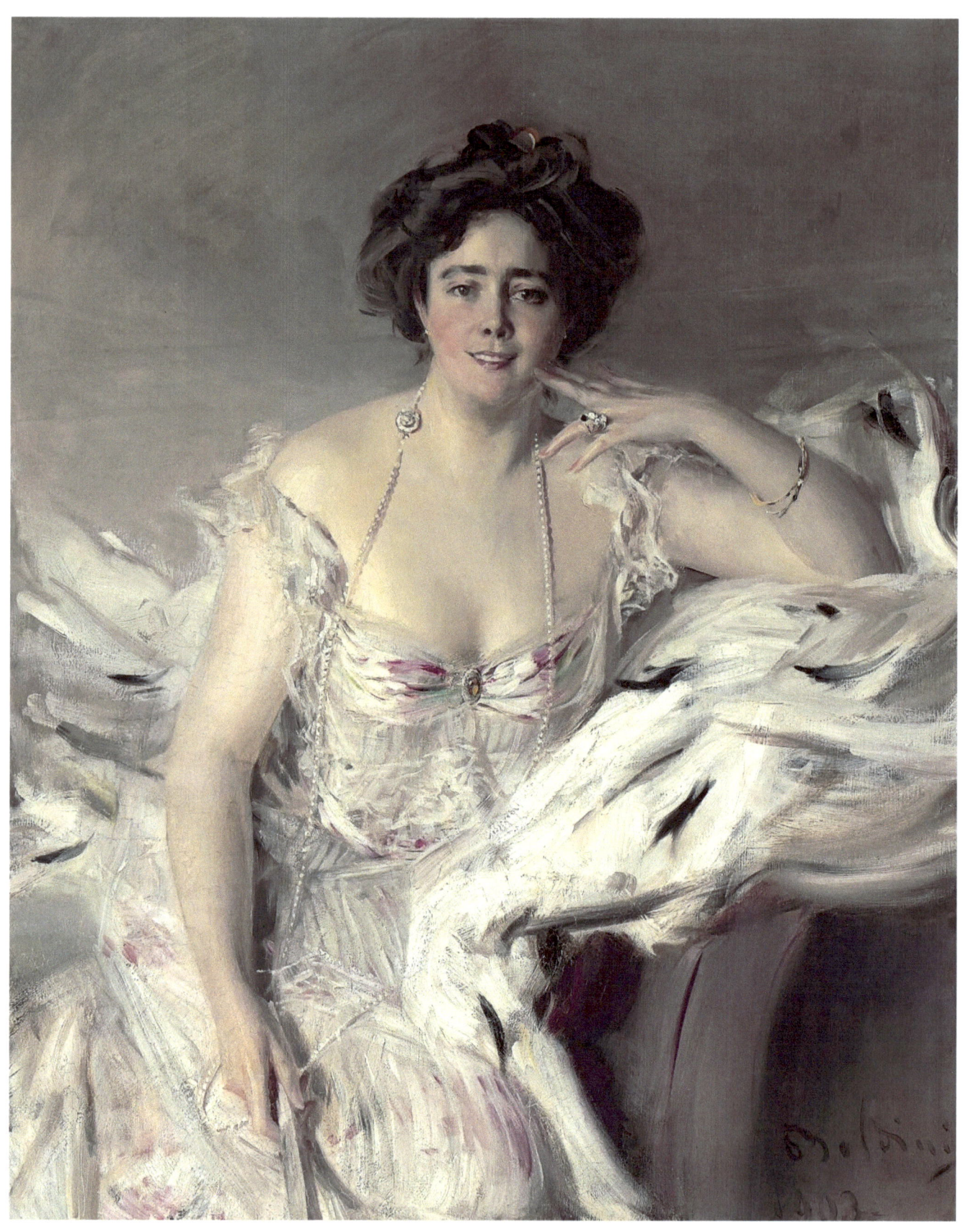

Lady Nanne Schrader

Oil on canvas

www.ingramcontent.com/pod-product-compliance
Lightning Source LLC
Chambersburg PA
CBHW050905180526
45159CB00007B/2799